Learn Java

A Crash Course Guide

to Learn Java in 1 Week

Timothy C.Needham

Timothy C.Needham

This document is geared towards providing exact and reliable information in regards to the topic and issue covered. The publication is sold with the idea that the publisher is not required to render accounting, officially permitted, or otherwise, qualified services. If advice is necessary, legal or professional, a practiced individual in the profession should be ordered.

- From a Declaration of Principles which was accepted and approved equally by a Committee of the American Bar Association and a Committee of Publishers and Associations.

The information provided herein is stated to be truthful and consistent, in that any liability, in terms of inattention or otherwise, by any usage or abuse of any policies, processes, or directions contained within is the solitary and utter responsibility of the recipient reader. Under no circumstances will any legal responsibility or blame be held against the publisher for any reparation, damages, or monetary loss due to the information herein, either directly or indirectly.

Respective authors own all copyrights not held by the publisher.

The information herein is offered for informational purposes solely, and is universal as so. The presentation of the information is without contract or any type of guarantee assurance.

The trademarks that are used are without any consent, and the publication of the trademark is without permission or backing by the trademark owner. All trademarks and brands within this book are for clarifying purposes only and are the owned by the owners themselves, not affiliated with this document.

Table of Contents

Introduction

I want to thank you and congratulate you for buying the book, *"Java for Beginners: A Crash Course Guide to Learn Java in 1 Week."*

This book is the ultimate beginners' crash course to Java programming, as it will help you learn enough about the language in as little as 1 week!

We all have dreams. My dream could be to become a great teacher, and chances are that your dream is to have a great career in IT or develop your skills and knowledge in IT for self-fulfillment (or something close to that). Without a doubt, the hands-on experience and expertise Java Programming Language offers is an essential requirement for anyone who's ardent about becoming a professional programmer.

But while you might be motivated enough to learn the language, I'm sure you must have asked yourself some questions severally: *why programming? Or why choose Java?* There are many reasons as to why you should learn programming- and Java in particular- most of which I'm sure you already know. If you ask me though, I'd be mean enough to say that some of us learn to earn. There are definitely many self-actualization and fulfillment related benefits that come with learning the art and trade of programming but the fiscal benefits are simply too conspicuous to ignore.

For one, Java is arguably the most acclaimed skill and is in demand nearly everywhere. IBM, Infosys, Twitter, Netflix, Google, Spotify, Uber, Amazon, Target, Yelp, Square, and other big players are always in need of a great Java programmer. Going by PayScale.com (the website that offers information about salary), an average Java developer earns about $70,000 annually. As a pro in the field, you have the entire globe to work over, as the demand is never restricted to a particular geographical area.

This book is the ultimate guide specially designed to help you move from a person largely unacquainted with programming to a person who can actually teach the subject and complete good programming projects. Here's the cool part: you get to learn the whole thing in ONE WEEK! It is updated to the latest versions (8 and 10) and the main topics of what the book will be about include:

- Variables
- Conditions
- Loops
- Arrays
- Operators
- User input
- Classes
- Objects
- Methods
- Object Oriented Programming which includes:
  - ✓ Inheritance
  - ✓ Encapsulation
  - ✓ Polymorphism
  - ✓ Compositions

And much, much more! Let's begin our learning.

Thanks again for downloading this book. I hope you enjoy it!

Before we get to the specifics, let's start by learning some of the common terms that you will encounter as you learn about Java, whether in this book or in any other learning material.

Understanding the Lingo: A Glossary

While the following list is in no way comprehensive of all terms that you will come across when using and learning Java, it will give you a good starting point to ensure you understand what is being talked about.

- **IDE (Integrated Development Environment) -** this refers to a software application that offers you comprehensive facilities for software development or basic programming. It usually comprises built automation tools, source code editor and a debugger.

- **PATH-** in its general form (of a directory or file), path refers to the specific location in a file system.

- **Source code repository-** this refers to a file archive and web hosting facility in which a huge amount of source code for web pages or software is stored, either privately or publicly. They are usually used by open-source software projects as well as certain multi-developer projects to deal with various versions.

- **Refactoring-** this refers to a process of altering a software system in a way that it doesn't change the external behavior of the code, but improves its internal structure.

- **Unicode-** this refers to a 16-bit character encoding standard that is able to represent nearly all characters of well-known languages of the world.

- **Compiler-** a compiler is a special program that is tasked with processing statements written in a programming language, and turns them into code (or machine language) that is used by the computer's processor.

- **Heap-** refers to a part of pre-reserved computer main storage or memory that a process of a program can access to store data in a given variable amount that cannot be known until the program runs.

- **Syntax-** refers to the general set rules in a programming language that describe the combinations of symbols considered to be rightly structured programs in that particular language.

- **Constructors-** they are special methods that are called when objects are instantiated, or, when you make use of the new keywords.

- **Modifiers-** these are keywords in Java that you add to classes, variables and methods to change their meaning

- **Naming convention-** refers to the rule that you follow to determine what to name your identifiers like package, class, constant, method or variable and so on.

- **Object oriented programming (OOP) -** is a kind of computer programming in software design that allows programmers to define the data type of a data structure as well as the functions or types of operations that are applicable to the data structure.

- **Access modifiers-** also referred to as access specifiers, access modifiers are keywords that set the accessibility of methods, classes among other members. They are a specific part of programming language syntax that facilitates component encapsulation.

As I stated earlier, the above list is in no way comprehensive. It will however, prove useful at this point, as a larger list would have been overwhelming. You can always refer to this list if something is not clear.

With that in mind, let's start our learning. In case you are completely new to this, we'll start with the basics:

Java Programming: A Background

Before we get into Java programming, let's first make sure you understand what computer programming (or coding) really is.

What Is Programming?

By definition, programming is the process of building software, which is made up of instructions. These instructions are basically referred to as the *source code*. The *source code* is a set of written instructions that a computer understands. Throughout this book, we'll be using this concept so you need to understand it before we begin.

What does the source code really look like?

Code doesn't typically follow the rules of natural languages, such as English. Take a look at this small program to understand what I mean:

```
require 'open-uri'
require 'json'
FRONT_PAGE_URL = 'https://reddit.com/r/all.json'
front_page = JSON.load(open(FRONT_PAGE_URL).read)
top_post = front_page['data']['children'][0]['data']
puts 'The top post on reddit is:'
puts top_post['title']
puts top_post['url']
```

A computer actually takes everything literally- for instance, when you ask a computer if a number is even or odd, it will always respond with a 'yes'. Don't believe me? Take a look at the code below:

puts (5.odd? or 5.even?)

The code will display 'true', which is, technically speaking, right. The number 5 is either even or odd- even though that's not what I really meant.

Programming also entails Testing and debugging

When code is written, it has to be tested because just writing it does not guarantee that it is correct. The code could crash from time to time, or display incorrect results, freeze or any other problem like that. Professional programmers usually employ different methods to test their code to try to avert such problems.

Lastly, we have a term referred to as ***debugging***- this is the process of investigating a problem, diagnosing it and fixing it in source code- as you will soon find out in the course of this book, this is actually a skill in itself.

So, what is Java programming language?

Java programming language is a computer programming language that uniquely lets you write the computer instructions using English-based commands as opposed to writing them in the usual numeric codes. It is referred to as high-level language due to the fact that human beings can read and write it easily. Just like English though, Java has some rules, which determine how these instructions are written; these rules are referred to as its **syntax**. Basically, when the program is written, the high-level instructions are translated into numeric codes that are understandable and executable to computers.

So, Who Created Java?

Java was created in the early 90s by a man known as James Gosling for a company called Sun Microsystems (which is currently owned by <u>Oracle</u>). The program was originally called Oak, and then Green.

Java was originally designed to be used to program home appliances controlled by different computer processors and then later, mobile devices like cell phones. Soon enough, there came the realization that the language needed to be accessible by various computer processors. In 1994, the language was seen as ideal for use with web browsers and in no time, its connection to the internet started. In 1995, the latest version of the Netscape browser capable of running Java programs was released by Netscape Incorporated and in 1996, when Java 1.0 was released to the public, its main focus had already shifted to use on the internet, thus offering interactivity with users by providing developers a good way to create animated web pages.

Since the 1.0 version, we have seen many updates and developments such as:

✓   J2SE 1.3 released in 2000

✓   J2SE in 2004

✓   Java SE 8 in 2014

✓   Java SE 10 in 2018

Java has undeniably evolved over the years as a great and successful language you can use on and off the internet. Let's touch on the benefits of using Java programming language:

The Benefits

Each programming language has been introduced with a purpose and has some benefits. Even though each language creates the opportunity to begin a flourishing career, Java is usually given preference. The benefits of Java in particular are indeed countless but I will mention a few briefly.

✓ *You get rich information*

While there is no obvious competition between existing programming languages, Java is considered the best-sometimes owing to its wealth of information. Java has been existing for many years so you can expect a quick answer to nearly all queries that come to mind with regards to programming. Thus, you can solve each one of your problems easily as you hone your skills in the process.

✓ *Ease of learning*

Sometimes beginners tend to think that the better a language is, the harder it's probably going to be to learn it. However, that is not true- at least not with Java. There are definitely some unavoidable initial hurdles but the fact that the language uses ordinary and simple English in place of generics or multiple brackets makes the language easy to learn. When you learn how to install JDK and the installation of PATH the right way, the rest will be fun to learn and implement.

✓ *You get a great toolset*

You will often hear that in programming, the toolset of a language has a major role to play in determining its overall success. Java undeniably has an upper hand in this respect because it comes with a complete support for *open source systems*. This means that as a user, you can get tools for nearly everything you require. We have a number of open source libraries that provide information on all topics to do with Java programming. Also, there are a number of communities- especially online to guide new programmers.

✓ *You get to learn from your mistakes*

We have a few languages that are designed to teach or allow you to learn from your own mistakes and let you build up your base. Java contains some great *IDEs (IDE refers to Integrated Development Environment* – see glossary) that are tasked with updating you of your errors as soon as you make them. Besides that, the language also suggests for you to reformat the codes and gives you the reason for doing that. That way, you get a clear understanding of coding right from the basic stage and barely get yourself making any mistakes as you begin your journey as a professional.

✓ *The language is free*

To get Java, you don't have to incur any cost from the very beginning. Therefore, whether you are in the learning stage or professional stage, you can create or develop an application using Java without paying anybody any cash at all. All you need to learn is how to get the program, set it up and begin.

✓ *Better scope for the professionals*

As you intend to learn a programming language to start a professional career, Java remains your best bet. It is applied in most existing apps and its scope is still being increased further. Therefore, by learning this language, you can expect a better career in the industry compared to another programmer specialized in another language.

With all that in mind, let's move on to actually getting started with Java.

The Fundamentals/Prerequisites

This section describes the things you need to get before you begin coding anything. To get started, you should download Java (Java runtime environment -JRE/ Java Development Kit-JDK), and the Integrated Development Environment -IDE.

How To Download And Install Java

Downloading and installing Java is simple for any kind of operating system. I will show you how you can download and install this program using Linux and Windows operating systems as examples.

1: Linux

By the end of this section, you will have Java well installed and configured for your Linux machine- whether it's Debian, Mint or Ubuntu. I will, however, be using Ubuntu 14.04 for the duration of the guide and also mention the terminal and non-terminal ways of going about the process to help you follow in case you are a complete newbie.

You are going to be installing either Oracle JRE or Oracle JDK so you need to really understand the difference between the two.

Oracle JRE (Java Runtime Environment)

JRE is the minimum requirement to be able to execute a Java program. It entails the JVM (Java Virtual Machine), supporting files and core classes. In other words, when all you care about is running Java programs on your computer or browser, you'll install JRE.

Oracle JDK (Java Development Kit)

This is a software development kit that comprises the JVM, JRM (Java Runtime Environment), as well as the entire list of class libraries present in the production environment to build and compile programs. Thus, if you want to do some Java development, you'll require JDK.

Having said that, let's start.

Create the Java Folder

As an example, we'll begin by creating an empty folder called 'Java' for your JRE/JDK files in the directory /usr/local which makes the path of the folder: /usr/local/java. Get to the terminal and type the command below then press okay:

sudo mkdir -p /usr/local/java

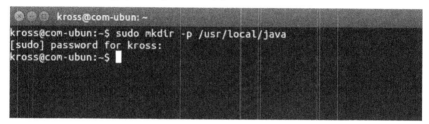

Check the Linux version
Before you download the java files, you have to understand the Linux version you are running (32 bit or 64 bit).

The terminal method

Open the terminal and type the command below, then press okay:

file /sbin/init

```
kross@com-ubun: ~
kross@com-ubun:~$ file /sbin/init
/sbin/init: ELF 64-bit LSB  shared object, x86-64, version 1 (SYSV), dynamically
 linked (uses shared libs), for GNU/Linux 2.6.24, BuildID[sha1]=7d9cc5d4d6cb68ae
de9400492a7c5942c55c7598, stripped
kross@com-ubun:~$
```

For instance, you can see in the above image that the result received before the command execution informs me that the Linux version I am running is 64 bit.

Try doing the same without the terminal:

Non-terminal method

As a user of Ubuntu, you can check your version by checking the *details* under *systems* panel in the *system settings*.

As you can see, the dialog box called 'details' will pop up. You'll see the Linux version beside the OS type in the 'overview' tab.

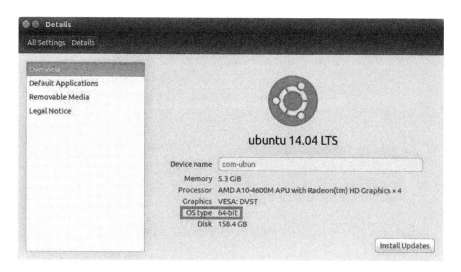

Download Oracle JRE/JDK

Head on to the Java <u>Download Page</u> and choose either JRE. Since you are only running Java programs on your computer (as I mentioned earlier) and don't require the full-featured Software Development Kit for Java in JDK (even though it also includes JRE) which is only useful for application development like android development, JRE (and not JDK) is good enough.

If you choose Java JRE, a screen like the one below will pop up. Just below Java SE Runtime Environment, you'll see 'Accept License Agreement'; check the box.

If you are running a 32-bit Linux, choose the Linux x86 link. If you are running a 64-bit Linux, choose the Linux x64 link.

The file will be downloaded to the directory: home /*unsername*/downloads. For instance, if your username is panda, it will be home/panda/downloads.

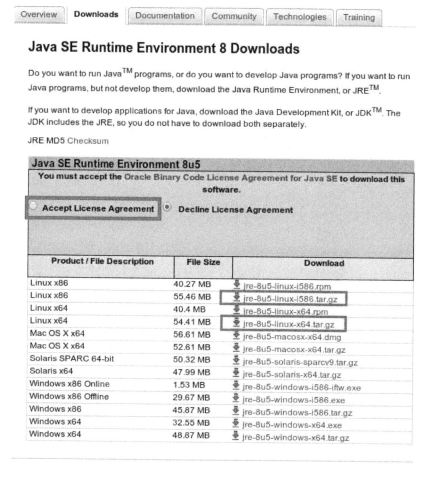

Copy the tar,gz JRE/ JDK files to the directory /usr/local/java

Type the code below and tap enter:

cd ~/Downloads

If you downloaded the 32 bit Oracle JDK, you will type the code below and tap Enter:

sudo cp -r jdk-8u5-linux-i586.tar.gz /usr/local/java

Enter the code below and tap Enter.

cd ~/Downloads

If you downloaded the JRE (32 bit), just type the code below and tap Enter:

sudo cp -r jre-8u5-linux-i586.tar.gz /usr/local/java

How To Copy The Oracle JDK (64-Bit) In A 64-Bit Linux

Like usual, type the code below and tap Enter:

cd ~/Downloads

In case you downloaded the Oracle JDK (64-bit), simply type the code below and press Enter.

sudo cp -r jdk-8u5-linux-x64.tar.gz /usr/local/java

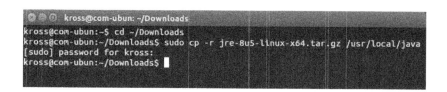

How To Copy Oracle Java JRE In A 64-Bit Linux

Type the code below and tap Enter:

cd ~/Downloads

If you downloaded the oracle JRE (64-bit), you can type the code below and press Enter:

sudo cp -r jre-8u5-linux-x64.tar.gz /usr/local/java

Extract the tar.gz JDK/JRE files to the directory: usr/local/java

Copying oracle Java in a 32-bit Linux

Type the code below and tap Enter:

cd /usr/local/java

In case you downloaded the oracle JDK (32-bit), simply type the code below and press Enter.

sudo tar xvzf jdk-8u5-linux-i586.tar.gz

```
kross@com-ubun: /usr/local/java
kross@com-ubun:~$ cd /usr/local/java
kross@com-ubun:/usr/local/java$ sudo tar xvzf jdk-8u5-linux-i586.tar.gz
[sudo] password for kross:
```

Extract the Java JRE (32-bit) in a 32-bit Linux by typing the code below, and then press Enter:

cd /usr/local/java

If you downloaded oracle JRE (32-bit), type the code below and tap Enter:

sudo tar xvzf jre-8u5-linux-i586.tar.gz

```
kross@com-ubun: /usr/local/java
kross@com-ubun:~$ cd /usr/local/java
kross@com-ubun:/usr/local/java$ sudo tar xvzf jre-8u5-linux-i586.tar.gz
[sudo] password for kross:
```

How about the Java JDK (64-bit) in a 64-bit Linux? Just type the code below and tap Enter:

cd /usr/local/java

For the Oracle JDK (64-bit), type the code below and tap Enter.

sudo tar xvzf jdk-8u5-linux-x64.tar.gz

```
kross@com-ubun: /usr/local/java
kross@com-ubun:~$ cd /usr/local/java
kross@com-ubun:/usr/local/java$ sudo tar xvzf jdk-8u5-linux-x64.tar.gz
[sudo] password for kross:
```

Extract the oracle Java JRE (64-bit) in a 64-bit Linux by typing the code below:

cd /usr/local/java

If you have the oracle JRE (64-bit), just type the code below and tap Enter:

sudo tar xvzf jre-8u5-linux-x64.tar.gz

```
kross@com-ubun: /usr/local/java
kross@com-ubun:~$ cd /usr/local/java
kross@com-ubun:/usr/local/java$ sudo tar xvzf jre-8u5-linux-x64.tar.gz
[sudo] password for kross:
```

Edit the system path

Start by opening the terminal and typing the following:

sudo gedit /etc/profile

By doing so, you'll have opened a text editor that has all the Linux system wide and startup programs.

Scroll down all the way to the end of the file and append the lines below to the end of the /etc/profile file:

If you're dealing with JDK, just add the code below:

JAVA_HOME=/usr/local/java/jdk1.8.0_05

PATH=$PATH:$HOME/bin:$JAVA_HOME/bin

JRE_HOME=/usr/local/java/jdk1.7.0_05/jre

PATH=$PATH:$HOME/bin:$JRE_HOME/bin

export JAVA_HOME

export JRE_HOME

export PATH

```
*profile (/etc) - gedit
File  Edit  View  Search  Tools  Documents  Help
   Open       Save         Undo

  *profile  ×

# The default umask is now handled by pam_umask.
# See pam_umask(8) and /etc/login.defs.

if [ -d /etc/profile.d ]; then
  for i in /etc/profile.d/*.sh; do
    if [ -r $i ]; then
      . $i
    fi
  done
  unset i
fi
JAVA_HOME=/usr/local/java/jdk1.8.0_05
PATH=$PATH:$HOME/bin:$JAVA_HOME/bin
JRE_HOME=/usr/local/java/jdk1.8.0_05/jre
PATH=$PATH:$HOME/bin:$JRE_HOME/bin
export JAVA_HOME
export JRE_HOME
export PATH
                  Plain Text ▾   Tab Width: 8 ▾      Ln 32, Col 1      INS
```

In the instance you are installing JRE, you should write the code below:

JRE_HOME=/usr/local/java/jre1.8.0_05

PATH=$PATH:$HOME/bin:$JRE_HOME/bin

export JRE_HOME

export PATH

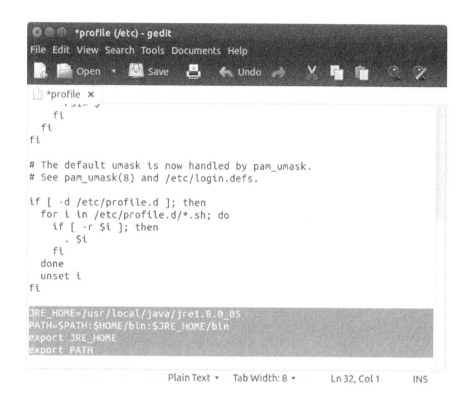

Save the file and exit.

Inform Linux about your Java's location

The commands below will let your system know that your java JRE/JDK is accessible or available for use.

For 32 or 64 bit JDK

In this case, just type the code below and tap enter.

sudo update-alternatives --install "/usr/bin/java" "java" "/usr/local/java/jdk1.8.0_05/jre/bin/java" 1

Type the code below and tap enter:

sudo update-alternatives --install "/usr/bin/javac" "javac" "/usr/local/java/jdk1.8.0_05/bin/javac" 1

Type the code below and tap enter:

sudo update-alternatives --install "/usr/bin/javaws" "javaws" "/usr/local/java/jdk1.8.0_05/bin/javaws" 1

For 32 or 64 bit JRE

If you are dealing with JDK, just type the code below and press enter:

sudo update-alternatives --install "/usr/bin/java" "java" "/usr/local/java/jre1.8.0_05/bin/java" 1

Type the code below and   tap enter.

sudo update-alternatives --install "/usr/bin/javaws" "javaws"
"/usr/local/java/jre1.8.0_05/bin/javaws" 1

```
kross@com-ubun: ~
kross@com-ubun:~$ sudo update-alternatives --install "/usr/bin/java" "java" "/us
r/local/java/jre1.8.0_05/bin/java" 1
[sudo] password for kross:
kross@com-ubun:~$ sudo update-alternatives --install "/usr/bin/javaws" "javaws"
"/usr/local/java/jre1.8.0_05/bin/javaws" 1
kross@com-ubun:~$
```

Make oracle Java JRE/JDK the default Java

If you are dealing with JDK, just type the code below and press enter:

sudo update-alternatives --set java
/usr/local/java/jdk1.8.0_05/jre/bin/java

Do the same (type the code below) for JDK and tap Enter:

\sudo update-alternatives --set javac
/usr/local/java/jdk1.8.0_05/bin/javac

Type the code below as well and tap Enter:

sudo update-alternatives --set javaws
/usr/local/java/jdk1.8.0_05/bin/javaws

```
kross@com-ubun: ~
kross@com-ubun:~$ sudo update-alternatives --set java /usr/local/java/jdk1.8.0_0
5/jre/bin/java
[sudo] password for kross:
update-alternatives: using /usr/local/java/jdk1.8.0_05/jre/bin/java to provide /
usr/bin/java (java) in manual mode
kross@com-ubun:~$ sudo update-alternatives --set javac /usr/local/java/jdk1.8.0_
05/bin/javac
kross@com-ubun:~$ sudo update-alternatives --set javaws /usr/local/java/jdk1.8.0
_05/bin/javaws
kross@com-ubun:~$
```

For oracle JRE (32 or 64 bit)

For the installation of JRE, type the code below and tap Enter:

sudo update-alternatives --set java
/usr/local/java/jre1.8.0_05/bin/java

For the installation of JDK, type the code below and tap Enter:

sudo update-alternatives --set javaws
/usr/local/java/jre1.8.0_05/bin/javaws

Reload the system path file/etc/profile

Type the following and tap enter:

. /etc/profile

You need to note that the system-wide path file will reload once you reboot your Linux system.

Test a successful installation

Open your terminal, type and tap enter: java –version

You get the something like this if your installation of 32 bit Java is successful.

```
kross@com-ubun:~
kross@com-ubun:~$ java -version
java version "1.8.0"
Java(TM) SE Runtime Environment (build 1.8.0-b132)
Java HotSpot(TM) 32-Bit Server VM (build 25.0-b70, mixed mode)
kross@com-ubun:~$
```

If you are using a 64-bit java, you'll get something like this:

```
kross@com-ubun: ~
kross@com-ubun:~$ java -version
java version "1.8.0"
Java(TM) SE Runtime Environment (build 1.8.0-b132)
Java HotSpot(TM) 64-Bit Server VM (build 25.0-b70, mixed mode)
kross@com-ubun:~$
```

If the tests mentioned above work as depicted above, you can be sure that your Java is successfully installed on your system.

2: Windows

The process of downloading and installing Java in Windows is even easier than in Linux. Let's go through the steps:

Click this link to download the latest version of Java JDK.

Java SE Downloads

Java Platform (JDK) 9

NetBeans with JDK 8

Java Platform, Standard Edition	
Java SE 9.0.1 Java SE 9.0.1 includes important bug fixes. Oracle strongly recommends that all Java SE 9 users upgrade to this release. Learn more ▸	
• Installation Instructions	**JDK** DOWNLOAD ↓
• Release Notes	
• Oracle License	
• Java SE Licensing Information User Manual	**Server JRE** DOWNLOAD ↓
• Third Party Licenses	
• Certified System Configurations	**JRE** DOWNLOAD ↓
• Readme	

Now accept the license agreement and download the latest JDK according to your version (that is 64 or 32 bit) of Java for windows.

When your download is complete, run the exe file to install JDK, and click next.

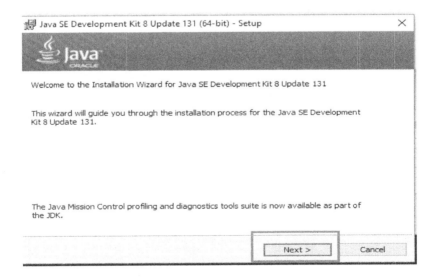

Click close when the installation completes.

Set Java environment variables: classpath and path

The path variable offers the location of executables such as java, javac and so forth. You can be able to run a program without specifying the PATH but you'll require a full path of executable such as ***C:\Program Files\Java\jdk1.8.0_131\bin\javac*** as opposed to the simple ***javac A.Java***

The variable 'CLASSPATH' provides the library files' location. We'll now look at the steps to set the CLASSPATH and PATH.

Right click on 'My Computer' and then select 'properties'

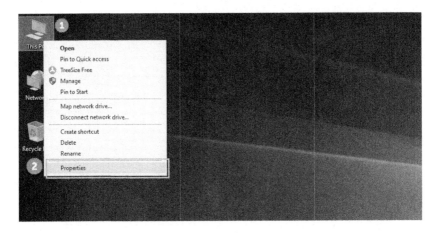

Select 'advanced system settings' and then 'environment variables'.

Control Panel Home

Device Manager

Remote settings

System protection

Advanced system settings

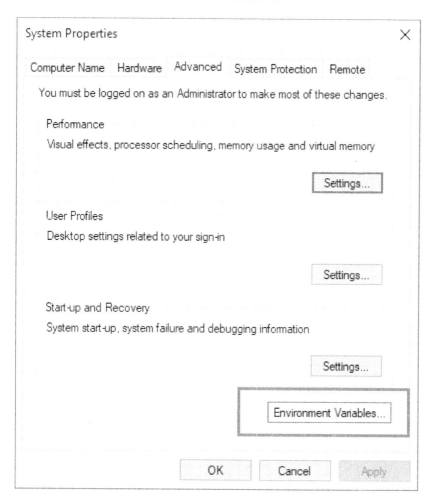

In the 'user variables', select the 'new' button.

In the 'variable name', type PATH.

Copy the bin folder's path that is installed in the JKD folder:

Paste the bin folder's path in variable value and then click on the 'ok' button.

If you have a PATH variable set in your PC already, just edit the PATH variable to the following:

PATH = <JDK installation directory>\bin;%PATH%;

In this case, the %PATH% joins the existing path variable to your new value

To set CLASSPATH, just follow the same process.

If you realize your installation is not working after you complete, just change the classpath to the following:

CLASSPATH = <JDK installation directory>\lib\tools.jar;

Now tap the 'ok' button.

Now go to your command prompt and enter javac commands. If the screen is similar to the one below, Java has been installed successfully.

Getting Eclipse IDE

An IDE (for Integrated Development Environment) makes you productive in development, as it helps you in handling important tasks such as coding, refactoring, debugging, running web apps and testing.

Nonetheless, the most important factor it offers- according to me, is speed (days of sitting around and waiting for stuff to compile or load are long gone). An good IDE such as Eclipse is extremely fast, doesn't suck up memory and takes short time to load, and doesn't take lots of time to synchronize changes. A good programming expert would also mention other features you get to enjoy such as 'integration with *code repositories' (see glossary)* and checking of errors- such as static code analysis and highlighting unused references.

Steps Of Installing Eclipse For Java On Windows
Download Eclipse

Go to this link and download the latest version:

Get Eclipse **PHOTON**

Install your favorite Eclipse packages.

Download 64 bit

Download Packages | Need Help?

Click 'download packages' under 'get eclipse photon'. As a beginner, you should select the fourth entry *'eclipse IDE for Java Developers'* (32-bit or 64-bit).

Click download.

The next step entails unzipping the downloaded file to install it. Unzip the file into a designated directory (for instance, c:\javaproject).

You don't need to run any installer. What's more, you can just delete the whole eclipse directory when you don't need it anymore (without having to run the 'un-installer'). Feel free to rename or move the directory. Also, note that you can unzip (install) more than one copy in the same machine.

Installing Eclipse on Mac OS X

Repeat the same process of downloading and installing Eclipse for windows explained above using <u>this link</u>. Just ensure to select Mac OS X (cocoa). When you select 'eclipse IDE for Java Developers', you'll get a DMG file. Double click this downloaded file (DMG) and follow the instructions given thereafter to install the program. The program will be installed in the location: /applications/eclipse.

Note that you may alternatively download a TAR ball (.tar.gz); double click to be able to expand into a folder known as 'eclipse' and then drag this expanded folder into the 'applications' folder.

Installing Eclipse on Ubuntu Linux

Install Eclipse for java by downloading from this page. As usual, download the 'packages' and for platform, select 'Linux', then 'eclipse IDE for Java developers' for Java SE program development. You will get a .tar ball in the downloads folder and the installation will be under /usr/local

```
1.  // Unzip the tarball into /usr/local
2.  $ cd /usr/local
3.  $ sudo tar xzvf ~/Downloads/eclipse-java-oxygen-2-
    linux-gtk-x86_64.tar.gz
4.      // Extract the downloaded package
5.      // x: extract, z: for unzipping gz, v: verbose, f: filename
6.      // Extract into /usr/local/eclipse
7.      // You can also unzip in "File Explorer" by double-clicking
    the tarball.
8.
9.  // (Optional) Change ownership
10.  $ cd /usr/local
11.  $ sudo chown -R your-username:your-groupname
    eclipse
12.      // Change ownership to your chosen username and
    groupname
13.      // -R recursive
14.
15.  // Set up a symlink to /usr/bin (which is in the PATH)
16.  $ cd /usr/bin
17.  $ sudo ln -s /usr/local/eclipse/eclipse
18.      // Make a symlink in /usr/bin, which is in the PATH.
19.  $ ls -ld /usr/bin/eclipse
20.  lrwxrwxrwx 1 root root 26 Aug 30 11:53 /usr/bin/eclipse ->
    /usr/local/eclipse/eclipse
21.  $ which eclipse

    /usr/bin/eclipse
```

To run Eclipse, just open the folder '/usr/local/eclipse' and then click on the icon 'Eclipse'; or just start a terminal and enter 'Eclipse'.

Lock Eclipse on the launcher

Just start the program and right click the Eclipse icon and then click lock to launcher. If you are using an older version (and thus the above is not working), just create a file '/usr/share/applications/eclipse.desktop' with the contents below:

```
[Desktop Entry]
Name=Eclipse
Type=Application
Exec=eclipse
Terminal=false
Icon=/usr/local/eclipse/icon.xpm
Comment=Integrated Development Environment
NoDisplay=false
Categories=Development;IDE;
Name[en]=Eclipse
```

You can now write your first Java program or project in Eclipse

Launch Eclipse (run 'eclipse.exe') from the Eclipse installed directory and then select an appropriate directory for your workspace- i.e. where you would want to save your files (such as c:\javaproject\eclipse for windows).

If the screen named 'welcome' pops up, click the button labelled 'cross' next to the 'welcome' title.

For all Java applications, you have to create a project to have all the classes (discussed in a bit), source files and important resources.

Do the following to create the project:

- Select 'file' menu then 'new', then 'java project' (or 'file' then 'new' then 'project' then 'java project.')

- The dialog named 'new java project' will pop up.

- Enter 'firstproject' in the 'project name'

- Check the 'user default location'

- Select 'use default JRE' in JRE.

- Check the 'use project folder as the root for sources and class files' in the 'project layout' and then push the button labeled 'finish'.

Before we continue (write our first project), let's go over some of the basic concepts of Java.

Basic Concepts In Java

Java Tokens

Tokens are basically the tiniest logical components of Java and any other program. The first step of the compiler is to separate the whole program into smaller bits known as tokens. You can think of them as the building blocks of a program.

Tokens are basically anything in a program that a compiler can identify during the compilation process or tokenization. Let's take a look at the types of tokens:

- Keywords

- Operators

- Literals

- Separators

- Comments

- Literals

Let's have a brief description of each one of them so that you get a better understanding.

Keywords

Keywords are special words or what are known as 'reserved' words in Java as they have a special meaning. We have a list of 50 keywords, which are highlighted below:

byte	short	int	long	double	float	char	boolean	void	public
private	static	import	package	class	interface	extends	implements	if	else
for	do	while	switch	case	instanceof	return	native	new	synchronized
strictfp	super	this	volatile	try	catch	finally	final	protected	transient
default	assert	break	continue	throw	throws	goto	abstract	const	enum

Identifiers

Identifiers are those names programmers use in program to any method, class, variable, packages, objects, labels or interfaces in Java programs (you'll learn more on the meaning of these terms in due course).

We have *rules of naming identifiers,* which include the following

- You cannot have any special symbols in Java identifiers apart from the dollar sign $ and the underscore (_)

- Identifiers need to begin from digits

- The keywords are reserved already and contain special meaning – so they can't be used as identifiers.

- The reserved literals are also allowed as identifiers; for instance- null, false and true

- You cannot use one name for multiple identifiers. Identifiers also have to be case-sensitive thus the Mf and mf variables are very different.

Some good examples of valid identifiers in this case include the following:

pasa 1, Name, roll_no, $raju, string

Invalid identifiers would   include something like:

45

True (reserved literal), Roll-no (a special character has been used), 16sita (begins with a number) and try (this is a java keyword).

NOTE: reserved literals and keywords in Java are those words you cannot use as variables or function names.

Operators

Operators are the symbols you'll use to produce some result as you apply with some operands. We have different types of operators in Java. As you will note, some strings can also be used as operators. Essentially operators are important in Java when it comes to building expressions and statements – some of them include: -, +, *, =, >= and so forth.

Separators

Separators are also referred to as punctuators. These special characters and symbols separate different parts of code from others. Sometimes, they connect and separate either one or multiple tokens or organize a code block – that's why we call them separators.

In Java, punctuators that are used include semi-colon (;), period (.), comma (,), pair of square brackets (**[,]**), group of parenthesis (**(,)**), pair of braces (**{,}**).

Literals

Literals refer to any values in Java programming that don't change in the process of program execution. You can think of them as constants for literals. These are constant values of some string type or primitive type. Any literal that is used in Java needs to be one of the types mentioned below:

• *Character*

This is what stores the Character constants in the memory. It basically takes up a size of 2 bytes but can hold only one

46

character since char stores Unicode sets of characters. It contains a maximum value of 65,535 and a minimum of 0.

- *Integer*

Integer types can basically hold whole numbers like -96 and 123. The values sizes that can be stored mainly depends on the type of integer we select.

Type	Size	Range of values that can be stored
byte	1 byte	- 128 to 127
short	2 bytes	- 32768 to 32767
int	4 bytes	- 2,147,483,648 to 2,147,483,647
long	8 bytes	9,223,372,036,854,775,808 to 9,223,372,036,854,755,807

This calculation – (2^{n-1}) to (2^{n-1}) −1 is used for the range of values. Here, n represents the number of bits required- for instance, the byte data type requires 1 byte= 8 bits. Thus, the range of values, which can be kept in the byte data type is as follows:

$$-(2^{8-1}) \text{ to } (2^{8-1})-1= -2^7 \text{ to } (2^7) -1$$

- *Floating point numbers/data types*

These are data types we use to denote the numbers with a fractional part. The single precision floating point numbers usually use up 4 bytes while the double precision floating point numbers use up 8 bytes. We have two sub-types here:

Type	Size	Range of values that can be stored
float	4 bytes	3.4e- 038 to 3.4e+038
double	8 bytes	1.7e- 308 to 1.7e+038

47

- *Boolean*

The Boolean data types basically store values with two states: false or true

Take the examples below to understand better:

- 34.43

- 5322

- 'd'

- Null

- True

Comments

In Java, comments are used in the process of documentation. Some people don't place comments in the category of tokens because the compilers usually ignore them during tokenization.

In Java, multi-line comments begin with the following:

```
/* ...
```

The single line comments begin with:

```
//....
```

What we've discussed is just a basic overview of Java tokens. I hope you understood what tokens mean. Let's now write a little java program and separate it into distinct tokens that specify their token type:

```
class Test{
    public static void main(String args[]){
      int w,x=10,y=20;
      w=x+y; // This line add x and y, then assign to w
  }
}
```

In the program written above,

•   The keywords include public, class, void, static and int.

•   The identifiers include: Test, main, args, x, w

•   The operators include: + and =

•   The literals include: 20 and 10

The separators include:

{, (...

The comment is described by: //this line add x and y...

As you can see here, the compiler breaks down the program into tinier logical individual parts known as tokens.

Variables

Variables are *containers* that store data in programming. When a variable is declared, it is initialized with some value and then changed to another value later on. A variable can be further used to do any calculations, printing and so forth. Each variable needs to have a datatype such as Boolean, int and so on, and that type needs to be specified at the time the variable was declared. Each variable needs to have a non-duplicate or unique name to identify it.

Let's take an example of a student program. In such, we can have a single variable to store 'the student section', another one for 'student roll number' and so forth.

```
char section;
int roll_number;
```

In this case, 'char' is used to specify the variable's data type while the 'section' is used to specify the variable name. That's not all; 'int' is the datatype and 'roll_number' is the variable name. You can assign some value to a variable at the same moment it is declared, in a process known as initialization.

```
char section = 'C';
int roll_number = 76; //assign 76 to roll number
```

In this case, 'int' is used to define the variable data type while the 'roll_number' is defined by the variable name, where 76 is the variable's current number. As seen above, one variable- or roll_number in your program can store numerical data whereas another variable- or section can store the char data. The special keywords in Java signify the type of data that every variable stores. This means that we can actually declare variables with the types/keywords and initialize the variable's value.

The Types of Variables In Java

In Java, variables can be divided into four categories namely:

- Static variable

- Instance variable

- Method parameter

- Local variable

Instance Variable

Also known as non-static fields, instance variables are used to store states of objects. The variables that are defined without the static keyword, and are outside any declaration method automatically are object-specific, and are referred to as instance variables due to the fact that their values are instance specific and their values don't get shared among instances. Some people look at non-static fields as instance variables because their values tend to be unique to each class instance. For instance, the currentSpeed of a certain bicycle is independent from another's currentSpeed.

Further, you need to note the following:

- When a space is assigned for an object in the heap (see glossary), a slot for every instance variable value is made.

- These variables are made when objects are created using the keyword 'new' and destroyed when the object gets destroyed.

- Instance variables hold values that have to be referenced by multiple methods, block or constructor, or the essential parts of the state of an object that need to be present throughout the class.

- Instance variables could as well be declared within the class level right before use or after use.

- Keywords used to specify accessibility of a class or type and its members, which are also known as access modifiers could be given for different instance variables.

- Instance variables contain default values. For the numbers, zero is the default value; it's false for the Booleans and null for the object references. During declaration (or within the constructor), the values can be assigned.

- The instance variables are also visible for all constructors, block and methods in the class. Typically, it's recommended to make these variables private or access level. Nonetheless, subclasses' visibility can be provided for these variables using access modifiers.

- The instance variables can be directly accessed by calling the name of the variable within the class. Nonetheless, within the static variables – that is when the instance variables are offered accessibility- they need to be called with the fully qualified name. Let's take an example:

```java
import java.io.*;
public class Employee {

    // this instance variable is visible for any child class.
    public String name;

    // salary  variable is visible in Employee class only.
    private double salary;

    // The name variable is assigned in the constructor.
    public Employee (String empName) {
        name = empName;
    }

    // The salary variable is assigned a value.
    public void setSalary(double empSal) {
        salary = empSal;
    }

    // This method prints the employee details.
    public void printEmp() {
        System.out.println("name : " + name );
        System.out.println("salary :" + salary);
    }
```

From this, you'll get the following result:

name : Ransika

salary :1000.0

Class Or Static Variables

Also known as static variables, class variables are declared using the static keyword in a class, but outside a method, block or constructor. Regardless of the number of objects created from it, there would only be a single copy of each class variable per class.

Static variables are seldom used – that is besides being declared as constants. Constants are variables essentially declared as private/public, static and final. Constant variables will never change from their first value.

The static variables are kept within the static memory, and it is not common to use static variables as private or public constants. Static variables are actually created when the program starts up and killed when the program stops.

Visibility is similar to instance variables. Nonetheless, most static variables get declared public because they need to be available for the class users. The default values are similar to instance variables and for the numbers, zero represents the default value. It is false for the Booleans and null for the object references. The values can get assigned either within the constructor or during the declaration. What's more, the values can get assigned in distinctive static initializer blocks.

Calling with the class name is what is required to access the static variables –className.VariableName.

Lastly, if we declare the class variables as public static final, this essentially means that the constants or variable names are all in the upper case. Moreover, if the static variables aren't public as well as final, this means that the naming syntax is similar to the instance and the local variables.

Let's take an example:

```
import java.io.*;
public class Employee {

    // salary variable is a private static variable
    private static double salary;

    // DEPARTMENT is a constant
    public static final String DEPARTMENT = "Development ";

    public static void main(String args[]) {
      salary = 1000;
      System.out.println(DEPARTMENT + "average salary:" + salary);
    }
}
```

The following result will be given:

-Development average salary: 1000

You need to note that if the variables are accessed from an outside class, the constant needs to be accessed as the Employee Department.

Local Variables

Local variables are used to store a method in its temporary state. The syntax used to declare a local variable is the same as declaring a field- for instance, int count=0;. You won't find a particular keyword that designates a variable as local as such a determination comes entirely from the location in which the variable is declared- that is between the method's closing and opening braces. Thus, local variables can only be seen by the methods, which they are declared in- so they cannot be accessed from the rest of class.

In short, local variables are referred to as 'local' because they can only be referenced and locally used in the method that they are declared in. Below is a method where 'miles' is a local variable.

```
private static double convertKmToMi(double kilometers) {

    double miles = kilometers * MILES_PER_KILOMETER;

    return miles;

}
```

Parameters

Parameters are also methods passed in Methods. For instance, in the main method, the string args [] variables is a parameter.

```
1. package com.jbt;
2.
3. /*
4. * Here we will discuss about different type of Varia
   available in Java
5. */
6. public class VariablesInJava {
7.
8. public static void main(String args[]) {
9. System.out.println("Hello");
10. }
11. }
```

Conditional Statements In Java

Every day in life, we come in contact with different kinds of objects as you try to get things done; at the same time, we use these objects to carry out different tasks. The one type of objects we tend to come in contact with are digital or analog devices such as phones, computers, cars, self-opening doors in malls and offices, and televisions.

In relation to the example above, you'll realize that the concept of conditional statements in Java depicts the way we go about our daily lives. Conditional statements, with regards to Java programming, are all about making decisions that are directed towards a desired result. Each day, we make decisions, and for these decisions, we get particular result.

In Java programming, we have two types of decision making statements to use when programming a software or device that you can run on any device like the ones I've stated above. These statements basically assist the device and the device's user as well to do something according to a particular state or condition.

The IF-STATEMENT is the first conditional statement. You need to note that the if-statement contains three versions, which include the following:

- IF—STATEMENTS

- ELSE—IF STATEMENTS

- IF / ELSE STATEMENTS

Let's see how an IF-statement works using the first device we mentioned.

```
if(batteryIsLow) {
    // Alert the user to charge
}

if(phoneStorageIsFull) {
    // Alert the user to delete contents
}

if(softwareUpdateIsAvailable) {
    // Alert the user to download
}

if(incomingCall) {
    // Ring Ring Ring
}

if(userPressPowerOffButton) {
    // Alert the user that phone is going off
}
```

In Java, we use the IF-statements to check for a condition or state of the phone and when that condition happens to be true, the action thus becomes executed. If the condition is not true, nothing will happen. Now let's consider the phone; if the condition or state of the phone is battery low, then the phone will inform you to charge it. If the phone storage is full, you can get a notification is to fix it just the same way it informs you to download a software update when it's available.

The if/else statements

Let's now use the second device to see how the if/else statement on the other hand works.

```
if(loginPaswwordIsCorrect) {
    // Grant the user access
} else {
    // Deny the user access
}

if(batteryIsLow) {
    // Alert the user to charge
} else {
    // Shutdown
}

if(laptopIsInactive) {
    // Enter sleep mode
} else {
    // stay on screen active
}
```

When you look at the image above, you'll see that the 'if conditional' statements are extended to complete another action in the instance the first one is false. You can also define another action that can be completed (in the if/else statements) if the first condition isn't true – in this case, the first condition is false. The conditions above are quite self-explanatory since they are evident in our day-to-day use of computers.

The other version of these statements is known as:

The If-Statements

Let's use the device we mentioned third to look at how an else-if statement works.

```
if(temperatureIsHot) {
    // Turn on the Air conditioner
} else if(temperatureIsWarm) {
    // Turn on the fan
} else {
    // Turn on the heater
}

if(speedIsGreaterThan80km/hr) {
    // Switch to gear 3
} else if(speedIsGreaterThan120km/hr) {
    // Switch to gear 5
} else {
    // Switch to gear 1
}

if(carIsNotInMotion) {
    // Open all doors
} else if(carIsInMotion) {
    // Lock all doors
} else if(carIsMovingSlow) {
    // Leave all doors open
}
```

Besides the if/else, Java also lets you test other conditions by using the **else if** keyword. Let's take the first case as an example; you can see that once you test the first condition, it was decided to test for two more conditions which are likely consequences in our day-to-day use of air conditions. Basically therefore, we are able to give actions to be carried out according to any possible condition- with the java else if statements that is.

Switch case

Lastly, we also have the 'switch case', another type of conditional statements used in Java. Just as the name implies, it is some kind of a 'switch case' that controls a light bulb. Therefore, it essentially means that you can have multiple switches to act as conditions that light up different 'bulbs' (or perform actions). See the image below.

Using the last device mentioned, we'll take a look at how a switch case statement functions.

```java
int televison = 0;

switch(television) {
    case 0:
        // Off mode activated;
        break;
    case 1:
        // On mode activated;
        break;
    case 3;
        // Scan for channels activated;
        break;
    defualt:
        // Sleep mode activated;
        break;
}
```

When you look at the image above, it is pretty obvious that the distance needed to open the door automatically is stowed in the distance variable. Following the declaration and initialization of variables, the switch case comes next to test all possible distances that are having their corresponding actions. What exactly happens is that you store the major variable required to perform a certain action and then go on to include other cases that can carry out other actions.

You need to note that you don't always need to use a switch case for purposes of calling just a single specific method as you can use it to create a scenario where a number of actions can be carried out based on what the user desires.

The switch case can also have as many cases as required and additionally, the default statement can be used to perform an action in the instance the rest of the cases don't equal the action required. See the image below.

With the device I mentioned last, we'll be able to see how a switch case statement functions alongside a default statement.

```java
int televison = 0;

switch(television) {
    case 0:
        // Off mode activated;
        break;
    case 1:
        // On mode activated;
        break;
    case 3;
        // Scan for channels activated;
        break;
    defualt:
        // Sleep mode activated;
        break;
}
```

At this point, I'm sure you know how you can create conditional statements in Java. It's now up to you to go ahead and include it in your programs when you finally begin coding.

Loops In Java

In Java or any other programming language, looping is a feature that facilitates the execution of a set of instructions or functions recurrently as some condition evaluates to true. Java offers three ways to execute the loops.

Even as all the ways offer the same basic functionality, they usually differ in terms of syntax and the condition checking time.

While Loop

The while loop, to begin with, is a flow control statement that lets code to be repeatedly executed according to a particular Boolean condition. You can think of the while loop as repeating the IF statement.

while (boolean condition)

{

  loop statements...

}

Take a look at the flowchart below:

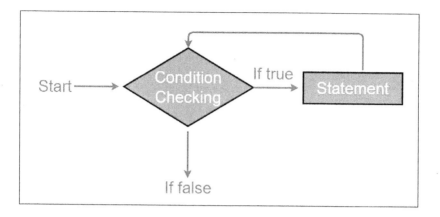

The while loop begins by checking the condition. If it evaluates to true, the loop body statements automatically become executed, if not, the first statement following the loop becomes executed. Therefore, it is for this reason that it is known as entry control loop.

When the condition evaluates to true, the loop statements get executed. Usually, the statements have what's known as an update value for the specific variable that is under processing for the subsequent iteration.

If the condition turns false, the loop then terminates thus killing its life cycle.

```java
// Java program to illustrate while loop
class whileLoopDemo
{
  public static void main(String args[])
  {
    int x = 1;

    // Exit when x becomes greater than 4
    while (x <= 4)
    {
      System.out.println("Value of x:" +
);

      // Increment the value of x for
      // next iteration
      x++;
    }
  }
}
```

When you run it on IDE, you get the following output:

Value of x:1

Value of x:2

Value of x:3

Value of x:4

For Loop

This type of loop offers a concise way to write the loop structure. Unlike the while loop, the for statement uses up the initialization, increment and decrement, and condition in one line, thus giving a shorter, easy to debug looping structure.

for (initialization condition; testing condition;

increment/decrement)

{

statement(s)

}

The flowchart is as follows:

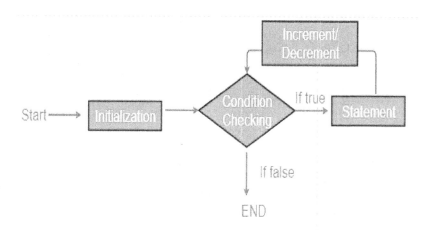

Initialization condition

In this case, you initialize the variable being used. It marks the beginning of a for loop. A variable that is already declared can be put to use or a variable can get declared, that is local to loop alone.

Testing condition

This one is used to test a loop's exit condition. It must take back a Boolean value. It also acts as an entry control loop as the condition gets checked before the loop statements are executed.

Statement execution

When the condition evaluates to true, the loop body statements become executed.

Increment/decrement

This one is used to update the variable for the subsequent iteration.

Loop termination

If the condition is false, what happens is that the loop terminates to mark the end of its lifecycle:

```java
// Java program to illustrate for loop.
class forLoopDemo
{
    public static void main(String args[])
    {
        // for loop begins when x=2
        // and runs till x <=4
        for (int x = 2; x <= 4; x++)
            System.out.println("Value of x:" + x);
    }
}
```

When you run it on IDE, you get the following output:

Value of x:2

Value of x:3

Value of x:4

The enhanced For Loop

Java also entails another for loop version that was introduced in Java 5. Enhanced for loop offers an easier way of iterating through the elements of a collection or array. It is rigid and you should use it only when you really need to iterate through the elements in a sequence without being aware of the index of the currently processed element.

for (T element:Collection obj/array)

{

   statement(s)

}

As an example (a demonstration of how you can use the enhanced for loop to simplify the work), assume you have an array of names and want to print all the names contained in the array. Let's take a look at the difference between these two examples. The enhanced for loop makes things easier in the following manner:

Running it on IDE will give you the following output:

Ron

Harry

Hermoine

Do while

The do while loop is largely the same as the while loop. The only difference however is that it checks for condition once it executes the statements and thus, it is a good example of the exit control loop.

do

{

    statements..

}

while (condition);

The flowchart is as follows:

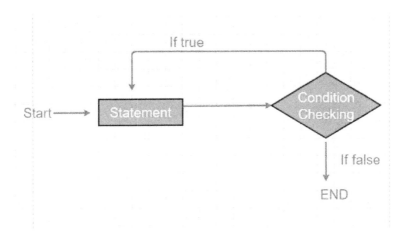

The do while loop begins with the statement(s') execution. For the first time, there usually isn't any checking of any condition.

Once the statements are executed, and there is the update of the variable value, the condition gets checked for a true or false value. In case it gets evaluated to true, the next loop iteration commences.

When the condition turns out to be false, the loop is terminated and just like that, its life cycle comes to an end. You need to remember that the do-while loop executes its statements not less than once before checking of any condition; therefore, it is a good example of the exit control loop.

```
// Java program to illustrate do-while loop
class dowhileloopDemo
{
    public static void main(String args[])
    {
        int x = 21;
        do
        {
            // The line will be printed even
            // if the condition is false
            System.out.println("Value of x:" + x);
            x++;
        }
        while (x < 20);
    }
}
```

When you run it on IDE, you get the following output:

Value of x: 21

With that, I think you are ready to learn something about Arrays in Java.

Java Arrays

When you hear the name 'arrays', think about a *container* that holds values or data of one type. For instance, you can have an array that holds 100 int type values. Array is an important Java construct that basically lets you store and conveniently access many values.

Declaring Arrays

Let me now explain how you can declare arrays in Java:

dataType[] arrayName;

In the example above, the dataType refers to a primitive data type such as char, int, byte, double and so forth or an object.

The 'arrayName' on the other hand is an identifier.

Let's look at the example above once more:

Double[] data;

In this case, data refers to an array that is able to hold values of the type 'double'.

How many elements therefore can this array hold? Since this hasn't been defined yet, our next step will be allocating memory for the array elements.

data = new Double[10];

The data array length is 10- this means that it can hold ten elements (in this case, it is 10 double values). You need to note that when the array length is defined, it can't be changed in the program.

We'll take another example:

int[] age;

age = new int[5];

In this example, the age array is able to hold five values of the *int* type. You can be able to allocate and declare memory of an array in a single statement. You can also replace two statements above with one statement.

int[] age = new int[5];

The Java Array Index

You can use indices to access the array elements- consider the (previous) example below:

int[] age = new int[5];

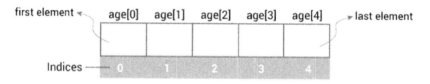

Array age **of length 5**

The initial array element is age[0], the second is age[1] and so forth. If the array's length is n, then the final element is arrayName[n-1]. Now that 5 is the length of 'age' array, the last array element is 'age[4]' in the example above.

Zero is the default first value of elements of an array for the numeric types; for Boolean, it is 'false'. This can be demonstrated as:

71

```java
class ArrayExample {

    public static void main(String[] args) {

        int[] age = new int[5];

        System.out.println(age[0]);
        System.out.println(age[1]);
        System.out.println(age[2]);
        System.out.println(age[3]);
        System.out.println(age[4]);
    }
}
```

Running the program gives the following output.

0

0

0

0

0

We have a better way of accessing elements of whichever array with the looping construct (the 'for loop' is generally used).

```
class ArrayExample {

    public static void main(String[] args) {


        int[] age = new int[5];


        for (int i = 0; i < 5; ++i) {

            System.out.println(age[i]);

        }

    }

}
```

How do you initialize Java arrays?

You can initialize arrays in Java during declaration or just initialize (changing values is also an option) later on in the program according to your need.

Initializing arrays during declaration

The following is how you can initialize arrays during declaration:

$$int[] \; age = \{12, 4, 5, 2, 5\};$$

This statement builds an array and then initializes it during declaration. An array's length is determined by the given number of values, which is divided by commas. In the example here, the age array's length is 5.

age[0]	age[1]	age[2]	age[3]	age[4]
12	4	5	2	5

We'll write a small program so that the elements of this array are printed.

```java
class ArrayExample {
  public static void main(String[] args) {

    int[] age = {12, 4, 5, 2, 5};

    for (int i = 0; i < 5; ++i) {
      System.out.println("Element at index " + i +": " + age[i]);
    }
  }
}
```

Running the program will give the following output:

Element at index 0: 12

Element at index 1: 4

Element at index 2: 5

Element at index 3: 2

Element at index 4: 5

How can you access the array elements?

It is easy to access and change the array elements with its numeric index. Take the example below:

```
class ArrayExample {
  public static void main(String[] args) {

    int[] age = new int[5];

    // insert 14 to third element
    age[2] = 14;

    // insert 34 to first element
    age[0] = 34;

    for (int i = 0; i < 5; ++i) {
      System.out.println("Element at index " + i +": " + age[i]);
    }
  }
}
```

Running the program will give you the following output:

Element at index 0: 34

Element at index 1: 0

Element at index 2: 14

Element at index 3: 0

Element at index 4: 0

An example of Java arrays

Below is a program that calculates the average and sum of values stowed in a type int array:

```
class SumAverage {
  public static void main(String[] args) {

    int[] numbers = {2, -9, 0, 5, 12, -25, 22, 9, 8, 12};
    int sum = 0;
    Double average;

    for (int number: numbers) {
      sum += number;
    }

    int arrayLength = numbers.length;

    // Change sum and arrayLength to double as average is in double
    average = ((double)sum / (double)arrayLength);

    System.out.println("Sum = " + sum);
    System.out.println("Average = " + average);
  }
}
```

Running the program will give you the following output:

Sum = 36

Average = 3.6

There are a few things here:

The *int* values, *sum* as well as *arraylength* get converted into *double* to calculate the average because *average* is *double*. This is known as type casting (see glossary). Getting the length of an array uses the *length attribute*. In this case, *numbers.length* returns the array: length of *numbers*.

Multidimensional Arrays

So far, we've been talking about one-dimensional arrays. In Java though, you can declare arrays referred to as multidimensional arrays. The following is an example to declare/ initialize a multidimensional array

```
Double[][] matrix = {{1.2, 4.3, 4.0},

    {4.1, -1.1}

};
```

In this case, matrix is a 2-dimensional array. Let's talk a bit about multidimensional arrays in Java.

The following is a 2d (two-dimensional) array. This array can be able to hold up to 12 elements of *int* type.

	Column 1	Column 2	Column 3	Column 4
Row 1	a[0][0]	a[0][1]	a[0][2]	a[0][3]
Row 2	a[1][0]	a[1][1]	a[1][2]	a[1][3]
Row 3	a[2][0]	a[2][1]	a[2][2]	a[2][3]

Don't forget that Java utilizes zero-based indexing- that means that in Java, indexing of arrays begins with zero and 1 the same way you can declare a 3d (three dimensional) array. For instance,

String[][][] personalInfo = new String[3][4][2];

In this case, the *personalinfo* is a 3d array that's able to hold up to 24 (3*4*2) elements of *string* type.

The components of a multidimensional array in Java are also arrays.

If you have some knowledge of C or C++ languages, you may have started thinking that Java's multidimensional arrays work the same way as those in C/C++. That is not the case though as Java's rows can vary in length.

During initialization, you'll see the difference.

Initializing a 2d array in Java

Take the example below to initialize a 2d array:

int[][] a = {

    {1, 2, 3},

    {4, 5, 6, 9},

    {7},

};

Each one of the array component 'a' is actually an array itself, and the length of all rows differs as well. To prove that, we'll write a program.

```
class MultidimensionalArray {
    public static void main(String[] args) {

        int[][] a = {
            {1, 2, 3},
            {4, 5, 6, 9},
            {7},
        };

        System.out.println("Length of row 1: " + a[0].length);
        System.out.println("Length of row 2: " + a[1].length);
        System.out.println("Length of row 3: " + a[2].length);
    }
}
```

You'll get the following output when you run the program:

Length of row 1: 3

Length of row 2: 4

Length of row 3: 1

Now that all the multidimensional array components are also arrays, it means that a[2], a[1] and (a[0] are arrays as well. You can find the length of the rows by using the 'length' attribute. Let's take a good example:

Printing all 2d array elements with Loop

```java
class MultidimensionalArray {
    public static void main(String[] args) {

        int[][] a = {
            {1, -2, 3},
            {-4, -5, 6, 9},
            {7},
        };

        for (int i = 0; i < a.length; ++i) {
            for(int j = 0; j < a[i].length; ++j) {
                System.out.println(a[i][j]);
            }
        }
    }
}
```

Note that it is better to utilize for...each loop when it comes to iterating through arrays when you get the chance. You can complete the same task with *for...loop* as:

```
class MultidimensionalArray {
   public static void main(String[] args) {

      int[][] a = {
         {1, -2, 3},
         {-4, -5, 6, 9},
         {7},
      };

      for (int[] innerArray: a) {
        for(int data: innerArray) {
          System.out.println(data);
        }
      }
   }
}
```

You will get the following output when you run the program:

```
1
-2
3
-4
-5
6
9
7
```

Initializing 3d arrays in Java

Initializing a 3d array is the same as initializing the 2d array. Take a look at the example below:

```
// test is a 3d array
int[][][] test = {
        {
        {1, -2, 3},
        {2, 3, 4}
        },
        {
        {-4, -5, 6, 9},
        {1},
        {2, 3}
        }
};
```

A 3d array is basically an array of 2d arrays. Just like is the case with 2d arrays, 3d arrays can vary in length. Let's take an example:

A program to print 3d array elements using loop

```java
class ThreeArray {
  public static void main(String[] args) {

    // test is a 3d array
    int[][][] test = {
        {
        {1, -2, 3},
        {2, 3, 4}
        },
        {
        {-4, -5, 6, 9},
        {1},
        {2, 3}
        }
    };

    // for..each loop to iterate through elements of 3d array
    for (int[][] array2D: test) {
      for (int[] array1D: array2D) {
        for(int item: array1D) {
          System.out.println(item);
        }
      }
    }
```

You will get the following output when you run the program.

1

-2

3

2

3

4

-4

-5

6

9

1

2

3

Java Copy Arrays

We're now going to learn about the various ways copy arrays (that is one and two dimensional arrays) can be used in Java. We have a number of techniques we can use to achieve this as explained in this section:

Using the assignment operator to copy the arrays

Take a look at the following example:

```
class CopyArray {

    public static void main(String[] args) {


        int [] numbers = {1, 2, 3, 4, 5, 6};
        int [] positiveNumbers = numbers;    // copying arrays


        for (int number: positiveNumbers) {
            System.out.print(number + ", ");

        }

    }

}
```

You'll get the following output when you run the program:

1, 2, 3, 4, 5, 6

Even though this particular method of copying arrays tends to work superbly, it tends to have a problem. The thing is, when you alter the elements of a single array in the above example, the other arrays' corresponding elements are also altered.

```
class AssignmentOperator {

  public static void main(String[] args) {


    int [] numbers = {1, 2, 3, 4, 5, 6};
    int [] positiveNumbers = numbers;   // copying arrays


    numbers[0] = -1;


    for (int number: positiveNumbers) {
      System.out.print(number + ", ");
    }
  }
}
```

You'll get the following output when you run the program:

-1, 2, 3, 4, 5, 6

When the initial element of the array 'numbers' becomes altered to -1, the initial element of the array 'positiveNumbers' likewise becomes -1. This is because the two arrays denote the same array object. This is known as shallow copy.

Nonetheless, we often require what's referred to as deep copy and not shallow copy. This (deep copy) copies the values to make a brand new array object.

Let's use looping construct to copy arrays

We'll begin with an example:

```
import java.util.Arrays;


class ArraysCopy {
  public static void main(String[] args) {


    int [] source = {1, 2, 3, 4, 5, 6};
    int [] destination = new int[6];


    for (int i = 0; i < source.length; ++i) {
      destination[i] = source[i];
    }


    // converting array to string
    System.out.println(Arrays.toString(destination));
  }
}
```

Your output will be as follows after running the program:

[1, 2, 3, 4, 5, 6]

In this case, the for loop is being used to iterate through each and every element of the 'source' array. In all iterations, the corresponding element of the 'source' array is copied to the 'destination' array.

The destination and source array do not share similar reference- that is deep copy. This means that id the elements of one array- either destination or source are altered, another array's corresponding elements are not changed.

The 'toString() method' basically works to change array to string - only for the output purposes. In Java, we have a better way of copying arrays (apart from using loops). This is by using the 'copyOfRange()' and 'arraycopy()' method.

How to use the arraycopy() method to copy arrays

The system class has the 'arraycopy()' method that let's you copy data from one particular array to another. The arraycopy() method is this efficient and also flexible. The method lets you copy a particular part of source array to destination array. Take a look:

public static void arraycopy(Object src, int srcPos,

Object dest, int destPos, int length)

In this case:

- Src is the array that you want to copy

- srcPos is the src array's starting position or index

- dest is the array which the the src elements will be copied to

- destPos is the dest array's starting position or index

- 'length' is the number of elements to be copied

We'll take an example:

```java
// To use Arrays.toString() method
import java.util.Arrays;


class ArraysCopy {
  public static void main(String[] args) {
    int[] n1 = {2, 3, 12, 4, 12, -2};


    int[] n3 = new int[5];


    // Creating n2 array of having length of n1 array
    int[] n2 = new int[n1.length];


    // copying entire n1 array to n2
    System.arraycopy(n1, 0, n2, 0, n1.length);
    System.out.println("n2 = " + Arrays.toString(n2));


    // copying elements from index 2 on n1 array
    // copying element to index 1 of n3 array
    // 2 elements will be copied
    System.arraycopy(n1, 2, n3, 1, 2);
    System.out.println("n3 = " + Arrays.toString(n3));
```

You'll get the following output when you run the program:

n2 = [2, 3, 12, 4, 12, -2]

n3 = [0, 12, 4, 0, 0]

You need to note that the default opening value of elements of the int type array is 0.

89

Using the copyOfrange() method to copy arrays

What's more, you can use this method that is defined in java.util.Arrays class to copy arrays. You don't necessarily have to build the destination array before this particular method is called. To learn more about this method, visit this page.

Let's see how you can do it:

```java
// To use toString() and copyOfRange() method
import java.util.Arrays;


class ArraysCopy {
  public static void main(String[] args) {


    int[] source = {2, 3, 12, 4, 12, -2};


    // copying entire source array to destination
    int[] destination1 = Arrays.copyOfRange(source, 0, source.length);
    System.out.println("destination1 = " +
Arrays.toString(destination1));


    // copying from index 2 to 5 (5 is not included)
    int[] destination2 = Arrays.copyOfRange(source, 2, 5);
    System.out.println("destination2 = " +
Arrays.toString(destination2));
  }
}
```

You'll get the following output when you run the program:

destination1 = [2, 3, 12, 4, 12, -2]

destination2 = [12, 4, 12]

Using loop to copy 2d arrays

Take the example below to copy irregular 2d arrays with loop:

```java
import java.util.Arrays;

class ArraysCopy {
public static void main(String[] args) {

    int[][] source = {
        {1, 2, 3, 4},
        {5, 6},
        {0, 2, 42, -4, 5}
    };

    int[][] destination = new int[source.length][];

    for (int i = 0; i < destination.length; ++i) {

        // allocating space for each row of destination array
        destination[i] = new int[source[i].length];

        for (int j = 0; j < destination[i].length; ++j) {
            destination[i][j] = source[i][j];
        }
    }
```

You will get the following output when you run the program:

[[1, 2, 3, 4], [5, 6], [0, 2, 42, -4, 5]]

As you can see, we've used the method 'deepToString()' for arrays here. This method better represents a multi-dimensional array as like in a 2 dimensional array. You can get more information about deepToString on this page.

You can use the System.arraycopy() or- in the case of one dimensional array- use Arrays.copyOf() array to replace the inner loop of the code above. Take a look at the example below that shows how to achieve the same thing with the arraycopy() method.

```java
import java.util.Arrays;

class AssignmentOperator {
public static void main(String[] args) {

    int[][] source = {
        {1, 2, 3, 4},
        {5, 6},
        {0, 2, 42, -4, 5}
        };

    int[][] destination = new int[source.length][];

    for (int i = 0; i < source.length; ++i) {

        // allocating space for each row of destination array
        destination[i] = new int[source[i].length];
        System.arraycopy(source[i], 0, destination[i], 0, destination[i].length);
    }

    // displaying destination array
    System.out.println(Arrays.deepToString(destination));
  }
}
```

Arrays are, after all, not that complicated! The next topic is even more straightforward. Let's take a look at operators to ensure some of what we've learned so far makes more sense, as well as what's to come.

Java Operators

Simply put, operators are characters representing specific actions. For instance, +, as you know it, is an arithmetic operator that denotes addition. In Java, we have the following types of operators:

- Assignment operators

- Basic arithmetic operators

- Comparison or relational operators

- Auto-increment/decrement operators

- Bitwise operators

- Logical operators

- Ternary operators

Basic Arithmetic Operators

These include things like +, %, -, *, /

- Addition is represented by +

- Subtraction is represented by –

- Multiplication is represented by *

- Division is represented by /

- Modulo is represented by %

You have to note that modulo operator returns remainder- for instance 10 % 5 returns zero

Let's take a look at some of the arithmetic operators examples:

```java
public class ArithmeticOperatorDemo {
  public static void main(String args[]) {
    int num1 = 100;
    int num2 = 20;

    System.out.println("num1 + num2: " + (num1 + num2) );
    System.out.println("num1 - num2: " + (num1 - num2) );
    System.out.println("num1 * num2: " + (num1 * num2) );
    System.out.println("num1 / num2: " + (num1 / num2) );
    System.out.println("num1 % num2: " + (num1 % num2) );
  }
}
```

The output will be as follows:

num1 + num2: 120

num1 - num2: 80

num1 * num2: 2000

num1 / num2: 5

num1 % num2: 0

Assignment Operators
The assignment operators include the following:
=, %=, +=, -=, /=, *=

- The operator that would assign the num1 variable to the va
num2=num1

- Num2 +=num1 is the same/equivalent to num2=num2+num1

- Again, num2-= num1 is equivalent to num2=num2-num1

- Num2 *=num1 is equivalent to num2 =num2 *num1

- Num2/ =num1 is equivalent to num2=num2/num1

- Num2% =num1 is equivalent to num2=num2%num1

Let's have an example of assignment operators:

```java
public class AssignmentOperatorDemo {
  public static void main(String args[]) {
    int num1 = 10;
    int num2 = 20;

    num2 = num1;
    System.out.println("= Output: "+num2);

    num2 += num1;
    System.out.println("+= Output: "+num2);

    num2 -= num1;
    System.out.println("-= Output: "+num2);

    num2 *= num1;
    System.out.println("*= Output: "+num2);

    num2 /= num1;
    System.out.println("/= Output: "+num2);

    num2 %= num1;
    System.out.println("%= Output: "+num2);
  }
}
```

The output you get by running the program is as follows:

```
= Output: 10
+= Output: 20
-= Output: 10
*= Output: 100
/= Output: 10
%= Output: 0
```

Auto-Increment And Decrement Operators

Here, we are dealing with -- and ++

Num ++ is equal to num+num+1 while num— is equal to num= num-1

Let's take an example of auto-increment/ auto decrement operators:

```
public class AutoOperatorDemo {
  public static void main(String args[]){
    int num1=100;
    int num2=200;
    num1++;
    num2--;
    System.out.println("num1++ is: "+num1);
    System.out.println("num2-- is: "+num2);
  }
}
```

The output is as follows:

num1++ is: 101

num2-- is: 199

Logical Operators

A logical operator is used together with binary variables. They are mostly used in loops and conditional statements to evaluate a condition.

Essentially, Java's logical operators are ||, &&, !

Consider the case that we have two Boolean variables: b1 and b2. In this case, b1 && b2 will return true in the instance b1 as well as b2 are true; otherwise, it would definitely return false.

On the other hand, b1 || b2 returns false in the instance b1 as well as b2 are false, otherwise else would definitely return true.

!b1 would, on the other hand, return the opposite of b1, meaning that it would return true in the instance b1 is false and return false in case b1 is true.

Let's take an example of these logical operators:

```java
public class LogicalOperatorDemo {
  public static void main(String args[]) {
    boolean b1 = true;
    boolean b2 = false;

    System.out.println("b1 && b2: " + (b1&&b2));
    System.out.println("b1 || b2: " + (b1||b2));
    System.out.println("!(b1 && b2): " + !(b1&&b2));
  }
}
```

The output is as follows:

b1 && b2: false
b1 || b2: true
!(b1 && b2): true

Relational Or Comparison Operators

In Java, there are six relational operators which include:
==, >, >=, <, <=, ! =

- In the instance the left and right side are equal, == returns true

- In the instance the left side isn't equivalent to the operator's right side, != returns true

- In the instance the left side is more/greater than the right side, > returns true

- In the instance the left side is smaller/less than the right side, < returns true

- In the instance the left side is more/greater than the right side, or equal to it, >= returns true

- In the instance the left side is smaller/fewer/less than the right side, or equal to it, <= returns true

Let's take an example of these relational operators:

First of all, you need to note that the example below is using the if-else statement, which you need to be well conversant with before you continue. You can refer to what we discussed earlier on this statement before continuing.

```java
public class RelationalOperatorDemo {
  public static void main(String args[]) {
    int num1 = 10;
    int num2 = 50;
    if (num1==num2) {
            System.out.println("num1 and num2 are equal");
    }
    else{
            System.out.println("num1 and num2 are not equal");
    }

    if( num1 != num2 ){
            System.out.println("num1 and num2 are not equal");
    }
    else{
            System.out.println("num1 and num2 are equal");
    }

    if( num1 > num2 ){
            System.out.println("num1 is greater than num2");
    }
    else{
            System.out.println("num1 is not greater than num2");
    }

    if( num1 >= num2 ){
            System.out.println("num1 is greater than or equal to num2
    }
    else{
            System.out.println("num1 is less than num2");
    }

    if( num1 < num2 ){
            System.out.println("num1 is less than num2");
    }
    else{
            System.out.println("num1 is not less than num2");
    }

    if( num1 <= num2 ){
            System.out.println("num1 is less than or equal to num2");
    }
    else{
            System.out.println("num1 is greater than num2");
    }
  }
}
```

The output is as follows:

num1 and num2 are not equal
num1 and num2 are not equal
num1 is not greater than num2
num1 is less than num2
num1 is less than num2
num1 is less than or equal to num2

The Bitwise Operators
We basically have six bitwise operators which include:
>>, &, |, <<, ^, >>,~

num1 = 11; /* equal to 00001011*/
num2 = 22; /* equal to 00010110 */

I'm sure you've heard that bitwise operators perform processing bit by bit.

Num 1 & num 2 essentially compare their corresponding bits (of num1 and num2) before generating 1- if the two bits are equal, otherwise, else would return 0. In the case here, it would return: 2 which is just 00000010 since in num 1 and num 2 binary form, it's only the second last bits that are matching.

Num 1 | num 2 compares num 1 and num 2 bits and then generates 1, that is if either bit is 1, otherwise it returns zero. In the case here, it returns 31, which essentially is 00011111.

Num 1^ num 2 on the other hand compares the corresponding bits of num 2 and num 1 before generating a 1; that is if they are not equal, otherwise it returns 0. In our example here, it would return 29, which is equal to 00011101.

-num1 happens to be a complement operator that only changes the bit from 0 to 1 and 1 to 0. In the example we have here, it returns -12. This one is signed 8 bit equal to 11110100.

Num 1 <<2 is a left shift operator, which is responsible for transferring the bits towards the left hand side and discards the bit that is far left, before assigning zeros to the rightmost bit. In the case here, the output is 44. This figure is equivalent to 00101100.

You need to note that in the example we have below, we are giving out 2 to the right hand side of the shift operator, which is the reason the bits are going 2 places towards the left hand side. You can change this number and the bits would have to be moved by the specified number of bits on the operator's right hand side. The same applies to the operator in the right side.

Num1 >> 2 is a right shift operator, which usually has a tendency of moving the bits to the right before discarding the far right bit, before then assigning the leftmost bit a value of 0. In the case here, the output is 2, which is equal to 00000010.

Let's take a look at an example of these operators:

```java
public class BitwiseOperatorDemo {
 public static void main(String args[]) {

   int num1 = 11;  /* 11 = 00001011 */
   int num2 = 22;  /* 22 = 00010110 */
   int result = 0;

   result = num1 & num2;
   System.out.println("num1 & num2: "+result);

   result = num1 | num2;
   System.out.println("num1 | num2: "+result);

   result = num1 ^ num2;
   System.out.println("num1 ^ num2: "+result);

   result = ~num1;
   System.out.println("~num1: "+result);

   result = num1 << 2;
   System.out.println("num1 << 2: "+result); result = num1 >> 2;
   System.out.println("num1 >> 2: "+result);
 }
```

The output is as follows:

num1 & num2: 2

num1 | num2: 31

num1 ^ num2: 29

~num1: -12

num1 << 2: 44 num1 >> 2: 2

That's pretty much what you need to know as regards to operators in Java. Before you continue though, you may want to cover ternary operator and Operator precedence in Java, which are not within the scope of this book, but are equally important.

Classes and Objects in Java

Some Basics Of Classes

Class or classification is a representation of an entity or something that is made up of behavior and state. The class' state is the data associated with it and the class behaviors are those actions the class can perform.

For instance, in classifying a simple vehicle, we can say that it has a model name, manufacturer name and a production year associated with it. You can also say that your simple car is able to accelerate and decelerate. In that case, you can define behavior and state with the rule below:

The class' state is simply what the class contains while the class' behavior is what the class is able to do. You can create a simple specification for your class using the example I've just given as follows:

```
class Vehicle:
  state:
    manufacturerName
    modelName
    productionYear
  behavior:
    accelerate
    decelerate
```

You need to note that nearly all the programming languages have a restriction on state entry names and behavior names from having spaces. For instance, *manufacturer name* isn't a valid state entry name, manufactuerName is. The latter name is written in what is known as the camel case, in which the first letter in lower case and the rest of the letters are capitalized.

We've achieved a basic description of a vehicle, even though it doesn't have enough detail to be deemed important. For instance, what action is done when you want to accelerate the vehicle? Here, our class' behaviors have been declared but are yet to be defined. A behavior declaration is a statement about the kind of behavior can be performed. The behavior definition is the statement about how the behavior is executed. For instance, adding a new state entry referred to as 'currentSpeed' enables you to define your behaviors 'accelerate' and 'decelerate'

```
class Vehicle:
  state:
    manufacturerName
    modelName
    productionYear
    currentSpeed
  behavior:
    accelerate:
      increase currenctSpeed by 1
    decelerate
      decrease currenctSpeed by 1
```

With the behavior definitions above, we are able to do some useful work with our class. As you would notice, the purpose of the behavior is altering the state of the class. This leads to a general rule concerning the class behavior: the purpose of the behavior allied with a class is either accessing or altering the class' state. This rule is very important – so much that there is a metric designed to measure it: *cohesion*. Cohesion refers to the extent to which the state of a class and behavior relate to each other and work towards a common goal.

Even though you know the way the vehicle accelerates and decelerates, you've only given a simplistic definition that does not account for an action that is unexpected. For instance, how about you begin with a current speed that is less than zero and decelerate? Generally, you should never be in a situation where the current speed is dropping below zero. This rule about the class state is known as an invariant. An invariant needs to stay true before a behavior is completed and afterwards as well. This logic can be supported by augmenting the current definition of deceleration like so:

```
class Vehicle:
  invariants:
    currentSpeed is greater than or equal to 0
  state:
    manufacturerName
    modelName
    productionYear
    currentSpeed
  behavior:
    accelerate:
      increase currenctSpeed by 1
    decelerate
      if currentSpeed is greater than 0:
        decrease currenctSpeed by 1
```

Types

We now have a more mature class specification, but don't have a major element. When you examine the current speed state entry, this deficiency becomes evident: what are the units for measuring the current speed? One kilometer per hour? One mile per hour? In this case, we've not even limited its value to be a measurement of distance per time. Given the specification, the vehicle's current speed could be in sloths units. We need to link a type with every state entry to be able to better specify our class.

Before supplying the types for the state entries, there has to be a connection that needs to be created: a class and type are one and the same. For instance, if you said that the current speed is a number, the number itself can be denoted by a class.

What exactly is a number?

Well, a number holds a value and has the ability to perform such actions as multiplying itself with another number or even adding another number to itself. You could essentially build a class specification for a number if you so wished.

```
class Number:
  state:
    value
  behavior:
    addWithAnotherNumber:
      update value to be value plus other number
```

Now that there is an understanding of the need for types, we can now update our vehicle class to have state entries that are properly typed (we'll use the 'type StateName' notation) where the name of the type precedes the state entry name.

```
class Vehicle:
  invariants:
    currentSpeed is greater than or equal to 0
  state:
    String manufacturerName
    String modelName
    Number productionYear
    Number currentSpeed
  behavior:
    accelerate:
      increase currentSpeed by 1
    decelerate:
      if currentSpeed is greater than 0:
        decrease currenctSpeed by 1
```

You need to note that a string is a sequence of characters and that we'll have to ignore the current speed units. It will, for the moment, suffice to limit the current speed to a number. As you go on to describe the types, you have run into two things that need to be addressed before continue adorning and maturing the vehicle class: the primitive and parameters to behavior.

Primitive Types

As you declare the state entries for the class in terms of other classes, we'll eventually come to a point where you can no longer reference another class without having a cyclical hierarchy. For instance, if you try assigning a type of 'number' to the state 'currentSpeed', how then do you define the class 'number'? If you try defining it in terms of other classes, how do you, therefore, define those classes? Since you cannot let a type system that accepts such infinite regression, you need to declare a value or values to exist. Such axiomatic types are known as primitive types.

Most programming languages have a basic set of primitive types which include decimal values (like single-precision floating point), integers, strings, characters and Boolean values (these could be true or false values). These types occur as a set of bits without the necessity to define a regressive structure of a class. Such primitive types can operate as building blocks to have more complex types in terms of classes created. For purposes of this discussion, we'll have to assume that the types 'string', 'number', 'Boolean' and 'character' exist.

Behavior Parameters

Another thing you have to look at is concerned with passing information to the class when you execute behaviors. For instance, when you want to accelerate to 80 kilometers per hour, you'd have to execute the accelerate behavior of the vehicle class successfully 80 times. That is definitely unruly for a real system. In place of that, you should try instructing the vehicle how much to accelerate by. For instance, when you execute 'accelerate by 30' and then 'accelerate by 15' gives you a speed of 45 kilometers per hour. To do this, you need to declare that your accelerate behavior can actually a value, which closely represents the increased speed as one of the parameters. For this, you'll border the parameter with a parenthesis before associating a type with the same notation as that for your class' state. As you would note, the parameter needs to be named, otherwise you would not be able to use or access the parameter inside your definition of the behavior. You also need to note that when a behavior fails to have any parameters, you'll use an empty set of parameters. For instance, if the 'drive' behavior doesn't take any parameters, its declaration will be 'drive ()'. As a result, you'll get the following class for your vehicle:

```
class Vehicle:
  invariants:
    currentSpeed is greater than or equal to 0
  state:
    String: manufacturerName
    String modelName
    Number productionYear
    Number currentSpeed
  behavior:
    accelerate(Number amount):
      increase currenctSpeed by amount
    decelerate(Number amount):
      if currentSpeed minus amount is greater or equal to 0:
        decrease currenctSpeed by amount
```

If right now you instruct the vehicle to accelerate by 30, you'd be able to increase the current speed of the vehicle by 30. Now that the value (30) is passed to your behavior at execution, it is referred to as an argument. Even though the argument and the terms parameter are closely related, you'll get a vital distinction: a parameter is a value referenced in the behavior definition. The argument on the other hand is the actual value passed to the behavior upon execution.

I deliberately selected the execution notation because it maps the arguments that are supplied to the declared parameters. For instance, 'accelerate(30)' maps the value (30) to *amount* (of the 'number' type) during execution. This parameters' notation can be extended for more than a single parameter by enumerating the multiple parameters in a list with comma-separation taking the form of 'doSomething(number valueOne, Number valueTwo)'. In instances when the arguments are positionally mapped, this very argument notation can come in handy- for instance 'doSomething (15, 37)' maps 37 to valueTwo.

Declaring Classes

Let's start with an example of a definition of classes:

```
class MyClass {
    // field, constructor, and
    // method declarations
}
```

This is a form of class declaration. The area in between the braces- or the class body- has all the code that offers for the life cycle of the objects made from the class- that is constructors to initialize new objects, the declarations for the fields providing the class' state and its objects, as well as methods to implement the behavior of both the class and its objects. The class declaration that precedes is a minimal one- it basically has all the required components of a class declaration. You can offer more information concerning the class, for instance, its super class' name, whether it implements any surfaces, and so forth, at the beginning of the class declaration. For instance:

```
class MyClass extends MySuperClass implements YourInterface {
    // field, constructor, and
    // method declarations
}
```

This means that 'MyClass' is MySuperClass' subclass which implements the interface 'YourInterface'. You can add such modifiers like 'private' or 'public' at the start- so you can see that the first line of a class declaration can get a bit complicated. Generally, class declarations can comprise the following components in order:

- Modifiers, like 'private' and 'public', as well as a couple of others that you'll come across later.

- The class name along with the initial letter conventionally capitalized

- The class' parent or superclass name, if any, with the keyword 'extends' preceding it. A class is only able to *extend* one parent.

- A list of interfaces separated by commas implemented by the class, if any which is preceded by the 'implements' keyword. A class can be able to implement more than one interface.

- The class body, bounded by braces {}

Declaring Member Variables

We have different kinds of variables:

- The member variables   in a class known as fields

- The ones in a block of code or a method known as local variables and

- Those in method declarations known as parameters

The class 'bicycle' uses the lines of code below to define its fields:

```
public int cadence;
public int gear;
public int speed;
```

The field declarations are made up of three components, which include:

- The zero or more modifiers, for instance, the *private* or *public*

- The type of field

- The name of the field

The 'bicycle' fields have the name *cadence, gear* as well as *speed* and all of them are of data type integer known as *int*. the keyword 'bicycle' identifies these fields as public members, which are accessible by any object able to access the class.

The Access Modifiers

The first and left-most modifier that is used enables you control what the other classes can access a member field. At the moment, you can consider *private* and *public* modifiers.

The *public* modifier has the field that can be accessed from all classes.

The *private* modifier has the field that can only be accessed within its own class.

In light of encapsulation, you'll find it common to make fields private, which means that they can only be accessed *directly* from the class 'bicycle'. Nonetheless, you still require accessing these values- something that can be *indirectly* achieved by adding public methods, which obtain for you the field values:

```java
public class Bicycle {

    private int cadence;
    private int gear;
    private int speed;

    public Bicycle(int startCadence, int startSpee
        gear = startGear;
        cadence = startCadence;
        speed = startSpeed;
    }

    public int getCadence() {
        return cadence;
    }

    public void setCadence(int newValue) {
        cadence = newValue;
    }

    public int getGear() {
        return gear;
    }

    public void setGear(int newValue) {
        gear = newValue;
    }

    public int getSpeed() {
        return speed;
    }

    public void applyBrake(int decrement) {
        speed -= decrement;
    }

    public void speedUp(int increment) {
        speed += increment;
    }
}
```

The Types

All the variables need to have a type. You can either use the primitive types mentioned earlier such as Boolean, float or int or just use the reference types such as objects, arrays or strings.

The variable names

All variables follow some conventions and naming rules, regardless of whether they were fields, parameters or fields. You need to keep in mind that the same conventions and naming rules are used for class names and method, except that:

- The first class name letter needs to be capitalized and

- The first word or only word in a method name has to be a verb.

Defining Methods

The following is an example of a typical method declaration:

```
public double calculateAnswer(double wingSpan, int numberOfEngines,
                double length, double grossTons) {
   //do the calculation here
}
```

The method declaration elements that are required include the return type, pair of parentheses (), name and a body in between the braces {} of the method. In general, the method declarations contain six components in order as follows:

- The modifiers like *private, public* among others.

- The return type, which is the data type of the value, which the method returned, or *void* if the method fails to return a value.

- The name of the method- the field name rules only apply to the names of the method as well but the convention is a bit different.

- The parenthesis-bound parameter list – a list of input parameters, which are delimited in commas that are preceded by their respective data types which are usually bound by parentheses. In case of no parameters, empty parentheses can be used.

- An exception list

- The method body that is enclosed between different braces- the code of the method, which includes the declaration of local variables comes here.

Two of the method declaration components contain the *method signature,* which is the name of the method and types of the parameter. The method declared above has the following signature:

calculateAnswer(double, int, double, double)

Naming A Method

Even though the method name can take the form of any legal identifier, the code conventions tend to restrict the method names. Conventionally, the method names need to be a lowercase verb or multi-word names that start with a verb in lowercase and then nouns, adjectives and so on. When it comes to multi-word names, the first letter of each of the second and following words needs to be capitalized. Take the examples below:

run
runFast
getBackground
getFinalData
compareTo
setX
isEmpty

A method typically has a special name within its class. Nonetheless, it's possible for a method to have the same name as the other methods, owing to method overloading discussed below:

Overloading Methods

Java supports overloading methods; the program can also differentiate between methods having dissimilar method signatures. This simply means that it is possible for the methods in a class to have the same name if they contain different parameter lists.

Assume you have a class that is able to use calligraphy to draw various data types- this includes intergers, strings and so forth- and that which has a method for drawing every data type. It is stressful to use a new name for all methods. For instance, 'drawInteger', 'drawString', 'drawFloat' and so forth. In Java, you are allowed to use the same name for all the methods of drawing but then pass a different argument list to each one of these methods. Therefore, the data drawing class could declare four methods with the name 'draw', each of which contains a different list of parameters.

```java
public class DataArtist {
    ...
    public void draw(String s) {
        ...
    }
    public void draw(int i) {
        ...
    }
    public void draw(double f) {
        ...
    }
    public void draw(int i, double f) {
        ...
    }
```

The type and number of arguments that are passed into the method helps differentiate overloaded methods. When you look at the code sample, the *draw (int i)* and *draw(string s)* are unique and distinct methods because they need different types of arguments.

You cannot declare more than one method that has the same name, the same type and number of arguments since the compiler is not able to tell them apart. The compiler doesn't typically consider the type when it is differentiating methods. This essentially means that you really cannot declare 2 methods using the same signature even if each uses a different return type.

Before you move to the next section below on creating objects, it would be great if you researched on these two sections as they are beyond the scope of this book:

- Providing Constructors for Your Classes

- Passing Information to a Method or a Constructor

Creating Objects

In java, objects are combinations of data and procedures working on the data available. An object contains a behavior and state. Both of these are kept in variables or fields while the functions or methods display the behavior of the object. The classes serve as templates to create objects. In Java, the keyword 'new' is used to create an object.

A class gives the blueprint for different objects. In this case, you make an object from class and each of the statements below from a program builds an object and assigns a variable to it.

Point originOne = new Point(23, 94);
Rectangle rectOne = new Rectangle(originOne, 100, 200);
Rectangle rectTwo = new Rectangle(50, 100);

The *point* class object is created in the first line; the second line and the third each create the rectangle class object. Each one of these statements is made up of three parts as described below:

Declaration- the code formatted to bold are variable declarations correlating a variable name with the object type.

Instantiation- like I mentioned, the keyword 'new' is an operator in Java that builds the object.

Initialization- a call to a constructor that initializes the new object follows the operator

How To Declare A Variable To Refer To An Object

You already know that declaring a variable requires you to write *type name:*

The compiler is this notified that you'll use 'name' in reference to the data whose type is 'type'. When dealing with a primitive variable, this declaration also tends to reserve the right amount of the variable memory. You are capable of declaring a reference variable on a line of its own- for instance: *point originOne;*

By declaring 'originOne' this way, its value remains undetermined until an object is created and assigned to it. The action of declaring a given reference variable doesn't stop at creating an object. To do that, you would need use the operator 'new' as I will describe shortly. You have to have an object assigned to 'originOne' before using it in your code lest you receive a compile error.

A variable in this state, which does not reference any object at the moment, can be illustrated in the following manner (the variable name and a reference not pointing to anything):

originOne

Class Instantiation

The operator 'new' allocates memory for a new object and then returns a reference to that particular memory to instantiate a class. You need to note that the phrase 'instantiation of a class' is no different from 'creation of an object'. By creating an object, you are building an instance of a class, thus, instantiating a class.

The operator 'new' needs one postfix argument – that is a call to a constructor, the constructor name gives the class name to instantiate. The operator 'new' returns a reference to the object it made. This reference is typically assigned to the appropriate type variable such as:

Point originOne = new Point(23, 94);

The reference that was returned by the operator 'new' doesn't require being assigned to a variable. You can also use it directly in whichever expression- take this example:

int height = new Rectangle().height;

This statement is discussed in a subsequent section.

Initialization of an object

Take a look at the code below for the *point* class:

```
public class Point {
    public int x = 0;
    public int y = 0;
    //constructor
    public Point(int a, int b) {
        x = a;
        y = b;
    }
}
```

This class has one constructor. You can recognize a constructor due to the fact that its declaration is using the same name as the class and it doesn't have any return type. The constructor that is in the class *point* takes two integer arguments as the code declares (int a, int b). The statement below gives values 23 and 94 as ones for those arguments:

Point originOne = new Point(23, 94);

When you execute this statement, the result is illustrated below:

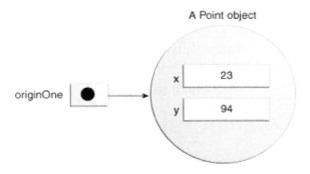

A Point object

The code for the class 'rectangle', which entails four constructors is as follows:

```
public class Rectangle {
    public int width = 0;
    public int height = 0;
    public Point origin;

    // four constructors
    public Rectangle() {
        origin = new Point(0, 0);
    }
    public Rectangle(Point p) {
        origin = p;
    }
    public Rectangle(int w, int h) {
        origin = new Point(0, 0);
        width = w;
        height = h;
    }
    public Rectangle(Point p, int w, int h) {
        origin = p;
        width = w;
        height = h;
    }

    // a method for moving the rectangle
    public void move(int x, int y) {
        origin.x = x;
        origin.y = y;
    }

    // a method for computing the area of the rectangle
    public int getArea() {
        return width * height;
    }
}
```

All the constructors allow you to give the initial values for the origin of the rectangle, its height, and width, with both reference and primitive types. In the instance a class has many constructors, they need to have unique (different) signatures. The Java compiler is able to differentiate the constructors according to the number of the arguments and their type. When this compiler comes across the code below, it knows to call the instructor in the class 'rectangle' that needs an argument 'point', which is followed by a double integer arguments.

Rectangle rectOne = new Rectangle(originOne, 100, 200);

This calls a rectangle's constructor, which then initializes 'origin' to 'originOne'. Moreover, a width is set by the constrictor to 100 and the height 200. You now have two references to the same *point object* – note that an object has the ability to contain many references to it, as you can see in the subsequent figure:

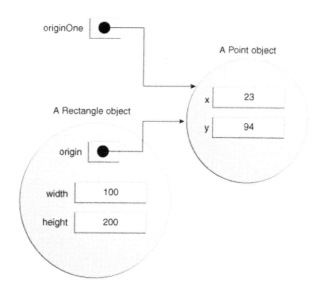

The constructor 'rectangle' is called by the line of code below-the constructor needs two integer arguments and they offer the initial values for the height and width. Inspecting the code inside the constructor enables you to see that it makes a new *point* object with x and y values that are initialized to 0:

Rectangle rectTwo = new Rectangle(50, 100);

The constructor 'rectangle' that is used in the statement below does not take any arguments, thus, it is known as a no-argument constructor:

Rectangle rect = new Rectangle();

All the classes don't have less than one constructor. In the instance a class is not declaring any, explicitly, the Java compiler will automatically give a no-argument constructor known as the default constructor. The default constructor usually calls the no-argument constructor of the class parent or the object constructor in case the class doesn't have another parent. If the parent doesn't have a constructor (the 'object' has one), the program will be rejected by the compiler.

As we draw closer to the end of the book, let's take a look at some cooler topics on object oriented programming that I'm sure will intrigue you!

Inheritance in Java

In Java, one of the principles of Object Oriented Programming is inheritance; inheritance lets us reuse existing code or extend a type that already exists or extend a type that is already existing. Put simply, Java allows a class to inherit another class and many interfaces, and interfaces are able to inherit other interfaces.

In our discussion today, we'll begin with looking at why you need inheritance and how it works with interfaces and classes. And then cover how the method or variable names and how the inherited members are affected by access modifiers, among other important things.

Why Inheritance?

Take a moment and imagine you are a car manufacturer offering multiple car models to your customers. While the different car models could provide features such as bulletproof windows or sunroof, they all have common features and components such as wheels and engine. It's only sensible to build a basic design and extend it to build their specialized versions instead of trying to design the car models individually, from scratch. Similarly, inheritance is here to assist you create a class that has simple features as well as behavior, and make its dedicated versions by building classes that inherit the base class. Similarly, interfaces are designed to extend the existing interfaces. You'll notice how multiple terms have been used to refer to a type which is under inheritance by another type: more specifically;

A base type is also known as a parent or super type

A derived type is known as a child or sub type, or an extended type

Inheritance With A Class
Extending a class

A class can inherit another class and define extra members. Let's begin by defining a base class known as Car:

```
1   public class Car {
2      int wheels;
3      String model;
4      void start() {
5        // Check essential parts
6      }
7   }
```

The 'ArmoredCar' class is able to inherit the 'Car' class members in its declaration with the keyword 'extends':

```
1   public class ArmoredCar extends Car {
2      int bulletProofWindows;
3      void remoteStartCar() {
4      // this vehicle can be started by using a remote control
5      }
6   }
```

In Java, the classes support single inheritance; the class 'ArmoredCar' cannot extend many classes. When the keyword 'extends' is not available, a class inherits the class 'java.lang.Object' implicitly.

What Is Being Inherited?

A derived class basically inherits (from the base class) the public and protected members –which are not static. Additionally, the members with package and default access get inherited in the instance the two classes are in one package.

A base class cannot allow its entire code to be accessed by the classes that are derived. A derived class static does not inherit the static and private members of a class. What's more, if the base class and derived classes become defined in isolated packages, the members who have package or default access in the base class don't get inherited within the derived class.

Access Parent Class Members -- From A Derived Class

Doing this is pretty simple; you only need to use them (you don't require a reference to the base class to be able to access its members). Take the brief example below:

```
public class ArmoredCar extends Car {

  public String registerModel() {

    return model;

  }

}
```

Members In The Hidden Base Class Instance

What if the base class and the derive class both define a method or variable that has a similar name? What happens? You should not worry in this case, as you can still be able to access the two. Nonetheless, you need to make your intent clear to Java, by prefixing the method or variable with the 'super' and 'this' keywords. The keyword 'this' refers to the instance which it is used in. The keywords 'this' refers to the instance which it is used in. The keyword 'super' denotes the parent class instance:

```java
public class ArmoredCar extends Car {

    private String model;

    public String getAValue() {

        return super.model;  // returns value of model defined in base class Car

        // return this.model;  // will return value of model defined in ArmoredCar

        // return model;  // will return value of model defined in ArmoredCar

    }

}
```

Many developers use the keywords 'super' and 'this' keywords to state the variable or method that they are referring to explicitly. Nonetheless, using them with all the members can make your code appear cluttered.

Hidden Base Class Static Members

What if the derived classes as well as base class and derived classes actually define different static methods and variables with the same name? What happens? Is it possible to access a 'static' member from the base class within the derived class, as we often do in instance variables?

We'll find that out in the example below:

```
1   public class Car {
2       public static String msg() {
3           return "Car";
4       }
5   }
1   public class ArmoredCar extends Car {
2       public static String msg() {
3           return super.msg(); // this won't compile.
4       }
5   }
```

No, you cannot. The static members usually belong to a given class and not to the instances. This means that we cannot use the non-static keyword 'super' in 'msg()'.

Considering that static members are usually belonging to a specific class, you can amend the prior call in the following manner:

return Car.msg();

Consider the example below, in which the base class and the derived class both describe a static method:

'msg()' with a similar signature

```
1   public class Car {
2     public static String msg() {
3       return "Car";
4     }
5   }
```

```
1   public class ArmoredCar extends Car {
2     public static String msg() {
3       return "ArmoredCar";
4     }
5   }
```

The following is how you can call them:

```
1   Car first = new ArmoredCar();
2   ArmoredCar second = new ArmoredCar();
```

The preceding code 'first.msg()' outputs 'car' and the 'second.msg()' simply outputs 'ArmoredCar'. The static message called relies on the variable type used in referring the 'ArmoredCar' instance.

Inheritance With Interfaces
Implementing multiple interfaces

Try to imagine the 'ArmoredCar' we defined in the earlier section is needed for a super spy. Thus, the company manufacturing the 'Car' thought it best to add floating and flying functionality:

```
1   public interface Floatable {
2     void floatOnWater();
3   }
1   public interface Flyable {
2     void fly();
3   }
1   public class ArmoredCar extends Car implements Floatable, Flyable{
2     public void floatOnWater() {
3       System.out.println("I can float!");
4     }
5
6     public void fly() {
7       System.out.println("I can fly!");
8     }
```

In the above example, you've noticed that the 'implements' keyword has been used to inherit from an interface.

Problems With Multiple Inheritance

Java allows multiple inheritance with interfaces. This was not an issue until Java 7 as interfaces could only be able to define abstract methods (those methods that lack implementation). Therefore, if a class implemented multiple interfaces using the same method signature, it wasn't an issue; the implementing class eventually had only a   single method to implement.

Let's now take a look at the way the simple equation changed when the 'default' methods in interfaces were introduced with Java 8.

Beginning with Java 8, the interfaces had an option of defining its methods' default implementation - that is an interface is still able to define the abstract methods. This means that when a class is implementing multiple interfaces that define methods having the same signature, the child class would actually inherit different implementations. This is not allowed just as it sounds complex.

Java doesn't allow multiple implementations' inheritance of the same methods that are defined in separate interfaces. Let me explain with an example:

```
1    public interface Floatable {
2        default void repair() {
3            System.out.println("Repairing Floatable object");
4        }
5    }
```

```
1    public interface Flyable {
2        default void repair() {
3            System.out.println("Repairing Flyable object");
4        }
5    }
```

```
1    public class ArmoredCar extends Car implements Floatable, Flyable {
2        // this won't compile
3    }
```

If you desire to implement the two interfaces, you'll have to override the method 'repair()'. If the interfaces in the earlier example are defining the variables with the same name- for instance, duration, you cannot be able to access them without having the interface name preceding the variable name:

```
1    public interface Floatable {
2        int duration = 10;
3    }
```

```
1    public interface Flyable {
2        int duration = 20;
3    }
```

```
1    public class ArmoredCar extends Car implements Floatable, Flyable {
2
3        public void aMethod() {
4            System.out.println(duration); // won't compile
5            System.out.println(Floatable.duration); // outputs 10
6            System.out.println(Flyable.duration); // outputs 20
7        }
8    }
```

Interfaces That Extend Other Interfaces

An interface can basically extend multiple interfaces as the example below explains

```
1    public interface Floatable {
2       void floatOnWater();
3    }
```

```
1    interface interface Flyable {
2       void fly();
3    }
```

```
1    public interface SpaceTraveller extends Floatable, Flyable {
2       void remoteControl();
3    }
```

An interface will inherit other interfaces by using the 'extends' keyword. The classes use the 'implements' keyword in inheriting an interface.

Inheriting Type

When a class inherits another one or interfaces, besides inheriting their members, it tends to inherit their type as well. This equally applies to an interface inheriting other interfaces. This is one very powerful concept that lets developers program to an interface- that is interface or base class- rather than programming to their implementations –either derived or concrete classes.

As an example, try to picture a condition in which an organizations is maintaining a list of the cars its employees own. All the employees definitely have different models. In this case, how can you refer to the different car instances? The solution lies in the example   below:

```
1    public class Employee {

2       private String name;

3       private Car car;

4

5       // standard constructor

6    }
```

Since all the Car derived classes inherit the type 'Car', the class instances that are derived can be referred with a variable of class 'Car'.

```
1    Employee e1 = new Employee("Shreya", new ArmoredCar());

2    Employee e2 = new Employee("Paul", new SpaceCar());

3    Employee e3 = new Employee("Pavni", new BMW());
```

Encapsulation In Java

Encapsulation refers to the ability to package related behavior in an object bundle and control or restrict their access in both function and data from other objects. It essentially is all about packaging related stuff together and keeping them away from external elements. You will note that keywords encapsulation along with data hiding are used interchangeably all over. You should not misunderstand that encapsulation is only about data hiding. When you say encapsulation, you should emphasize on grouping, packaging or even bundling related data as well as behavior together.

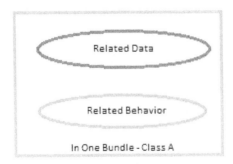

When you assign a class in object oriented programming, it is said that the first principle you should consider is encapsulation. Group the associated data and its behavior in a bucket. The main benefit of encapsulation is maintainability.

Believe it all or not, that's pretty much it when it comes to encapsulation! You can leave it as simple as that with nothing more or less.

Java Encapsulation

Any Java class that is well defined in its context domain is a good example for Java encapsulation. Thus, the essence here is basically for bundling methods and data together only after this data hiding is highlighted. The term data hiding in this case relates to the access specifiers in Java. It is easier to hide an attribute or method from the outer word by using the access specifier 'private'.

Therefore, hiding is quite plain and simple. But how about bundling method and data? This in particular is important. You have to understand well the business domain and design the class and group attributes, as well as its methods together based on that. This process is vital in encapsulation.

Take the Java encapsulation outline example below. When you talk about an animal, you should have all its attributes listed as well as its behavior such as how it will run, mate, hunt and so forth. When you bundle all these behavior and data in one class, you are essentially following the principles of encapsulation.

```java
package com.javapapers.java;

public class Animal {
        private String animalName;
        private String animalType;
        private int height;
        private String color;

        public Animal(String animalName, String animalType) {
                this.animalName = animalName;
                this.animalType = animalType;
        }

        public void hunt() {
                // implementation of hunt
        }

        public void run() {
                // implementation of run
        }

        public void mate() {
                // implementation of mate
        }
        //encapsulation is not about having getter/setters
        public String getAnimalName() {

                return animalName;
        }

        public void setAnimalName(String animalName) {
                this.animalName = animalName;
        }

        public String getAnimalType() {
                return animalType;
        }

        public void setAnimalType(String animalType) {
                this.animalType = animalType;
        }
```

NOTE: there is a line of difference between encapsulation and abstraction. You'll understand that easily with a simple example and the next tutorial on abstraction will give you a better insight into that. Just make sure to practice encapsulation as you design the classes.

Abstraction In Java

Abstraction is the situation where you hide the implementation details and only show the functionality; in Java, abstraction is achieved by use of interface and abstract class. Interface will give you 100% abstraction and the abstract will offer you 0-100% abstraction.

When you are in the streets and spot a nice vehicle on the road, you only get to see the entire picture; the car is only a single unit. You don't see the core of it: the complex mechanical engineering behind it.

Now imagine yourself going to a showroom to purchase a car. What are you seeing now? You are seeing a powerful engine, four wheels, and the steering wheel and so on. You can now see the car for what it really is- at its high components. But even so, we have so much inside it that gives the car its completeness. Now imagine you are the mechanic who's going to service the vehicle, you'll get to see it one more level deeper with another level of information.

When you design software, you need to take the context. In the example above, you ask the question as to whether you are designing the software for casual onlookers, purchasers or mechanics. In this regard, the abstraction levels is applied accordingly on the design.

Abstraction in Object Oriented Programming

Generally speaking, the software language itself is a good example for the concept of abstraction. When you write a statement in the following way:

a=b+c

You are adding two values that are stored in 2 different locations then moving ahead to store the product in a brand new location. You just describe it in a form that easily understandable by human beings. What goes on beneath? We have instruction sets, registers, program counters, storage units and so forth involved. We have POP, PUSH taking place. High level language that we use tends to abstract these complex details.

When we talk of abstraction in Java, we mean abstraction in OOP and the way it's done in Java. Abstraction begins the moment a class begins getting conceived. I cannot really say that restricting the properties of a given object using Java access modifiers can be termed as abstraction, as there is a lot more to it. You will find abstraction being used often in object oriented programming and in software.

Abstraction And Encapsulation

When a class becomes conceptualized, what are the properties you can have in it based on the context? If you want to design a class called animal and the context is zoo, you need to have an attribute as animalType to define wild or domestic. This attribute may not make much sense when you are designing the class in another context.

In the same way, ask yourself what behavior you are going to have in the class. Abstraction is applied here as well. What is important to have is different from what will be an overdose.

Cut off some of the information off from the class, and this process is using or applying abstraction.

When asked for the difference between encapsulation and abstraction, you can say that encapsulation applies abstraction just as a concept. Therefore, it is just encapsulation. But abstraction is a concept that is even applied as part of polymorphism (discussed later) and inheritance. You need to look at abstraction at a higher level among the other concepts of object oriented programming including polymorphism, inheritance and encapsulation.

Abstraction And Inheritance

Let's try to take inheritance in this discussion as well. When you are designing the hierarchy of classes, you apply abstraction and then create many layers between the hierarchies. Let's take a first level class cell as an example; next level will be LivingBeing and animal will be the next after that. The hierarchy you create here based on the context, which you are programming for uses abstraction itself. Now for each level, what exactly are the properties and behaviors that you are going to have? Abstraction also plays a very important role here in determining that. What are the common properties that can be exposed to a higher level in order for the lower level classes to inherit from it? Some properties don't need to be kept at higher level. This process of decision making is nothing but using abstraction to have different hierarchy layers.

Now that you read the short section, you should now have an idea about the way abstraction is done in Java.

• When you conceptualize classes

• When you write interfaces

- When you write abstract class methods

- When you write extends

- When you apply modifiers such as 'private', ...

You use abstraction as a concept in the areas identified above.

Polymorphism In Java

Polymorphism in its literal sense refers to a state of having many shapes or the ability to take on various forms. When it is used in an object oriented programming language such as Java, it describes the ability of the language to process objects of various classes and types through a uniform and single interface.

Polymorphism takes on two types: Runtime polymorphism and static binding (also known as compile time polymorphism). The former entails method overloading as an example while the latter is contained in dynamic polymorphism.

Perhaps you need to note that polymorphism entails a very important example, which is how a parent class refers to a child class object. As a matter of fact, any object satisfying more than a single IS-A relationship is by nature polymorphic.

As an example, we can consider the class _animal_ and let one of its subclasses be _cat_. Therefore, any cat is an animal. The cat in this case satisfies the IS-A relationship for its own type and also its super class 'animal'. You also need to note that it is very legal to state that every object in Java is by nature polymorphic because each one of them passes the IS-A test for itself as well as that for the 'object' class.

Static Polymorphism

When it comes to Java language, we achieve static polymorphism through something called method overloading. Method overloading simply means that there are a number of methods available in a class that have the same name but different types or order or number of parameters.

Java knows, at compile time, the kind of method to invoke by looking at the method signatures. Therefore, this is known as static binding or the compile time polymorphism.

Let the following example make this concept clearer for you:

```
class DemoOverload{

    public int add(int x, int y){ //method 1

    return x+y;

    }

    public int add(int x, int y, int z){ //method 2

    return x+y+z;

    }

    public int add(double x, int y){ //method 3

    return (int)x+y;

    }

    public int add(int x, double y){ //method 4

    return x+(int)y;

    }

}
class Test{

    public static void main(String[] args){

    DemoOverload demo=new DemoOverload();

    System.out.println(demo.add(2,3));      //method 1 called

    System.out.println(demo.add(2,3,4));   //method 2 called

    System.out.println(demo.add(2,3.4));   //method 4 called

    System.out.println(demo.add(2.5,3));   //method 3 called

    }

}
```

In the example above, we have four forms of 'add' methods. The first one takes two parameters and the second one takes three of them. The 3rd and 4th methods provide for a change of order of the parameters. The compiler usually checks the method signature after which it make a decision on which method to be invoked when compile time comes for a certain method call.

Dynamic Polymorphism

Imagine you have a sub class that is overriding a certain method of the super class. Imagine, you have, in the program, an object of the sub class created and have it assigned to the super class reference. In this case, if you call the overridden method on the reference of the super class, it means that the sub class version of the method will be called as a result. Take a look at the example below:

```
class Vehicle{
   public void move(){
   System.out.println("Vehicles can move!!");
   }
}
class MotorBike extends Vehicle{
   public void move(){
   System.out.println("MotorBike can move and accelerate too!!");
   }
}
class Test{
   public static void main(String[] args){
   Vehicle vh=new MotorBike();
   vh.move();   // prints MotorBike can move and accelerate too!!
   vh=new Vehicle();
   vh.move();   // prints Vehicles can move!!
   }
}
```

You need to note that in your first call to 'move()', the reference type is 'vehicle' while 'Motorbike' is the object being referenced. In this case, when you make a call to 'move()', the program will wait until it is runtime to determine the object that the reference is pointing to. In our case here, the object is of the 'MotorBike' class. Therefore the 'move()' method if the class 'MotorBike' will be called. The second call to 'move()' has the class 'vehicle' as its object. Therefore, the method 'move()' of the 'vehicle' will get called.

Note that at runtime, when the method to call is determined, this is referred to as late binding or dynamic binding.

As a recap, by now you should know that:

- In Java, an object that passes multiple IS-A tests is automatically polymorphic by nature

- In Java, all objects pass a minimum of two IS-A tests- that is one for the object class and one for itself

- In Java, static polymorphism is done through method overloading

- In Java, Dynamic polymorphism is attained through method overriding.

We discussed the concept of inheritance, which is undeniably a powerful mechanism when it comes to reusing code, improving the general organization of object oriented system and minimizing data redundancy. Inheritance is ideal when the classes are related to each other whereby the child class is essentially a parent class. For instance, a 'Car' is a 'vehicle' and as such, the class 'car' contains all the properties or features of the 'vehicle' class apart from its very own features. Nonetheless, you cannot always be having *is a* relationship in between object that are of different classes. Let's say with an example that 'a car isn't some kind of an engine'. You have an alternative referred to as composition to represent such a relationship. It is applied when the classes are related to each other in which the parent class is contained in the child class.

Composition basically makes a class reuse the functionality by making a reference to the class object that it wants to use- which is nothing like inheritance where a sub class extends the super class' functionality. For instance, a door has a button, a zoo has a lion, a car has an engine.

Composition is a special case of aggregation- this means that a restricted aggregation is known as composition. When an object has the other one (object) and the object that is contained does not exist without the other object, we can call that composition.

An example using a program

We'll consider a program that shows the concept of composition below. Follow the steps as indicated:

Step#1

We begin by creating a class 'Bike' which you can declare and define the data members and methods as follows:

```
class Bike
{

  // declaring data members and methods

  private String color;

  private int wheels;

  public void bikeFeatures()

  {

    System.out.println("Bike Color= "+color + " wheels= " + wheels);

  }

  public void setColor(String color)

  {

    this.color = color;

  }

  public void setwheels(int wheels)

  {

    this.wheels = wheels;

  }

}
```

Step#2

Now create a class called 'Honda' that extends the 'Bike' class above. In this case, 'Honda' class uses the 'HondaEngine' class, object 'start()' method via composition. You can now say that class 'Honda' has-a 'hondaEngine':

```
class Honda extends Bike

{

  //inherits all properties of bike class

  public void setStart()

  {

    HondaEngine e = new HondaEngine();

    e.start();

  }

}
```

Step# 3

Next, you have to create a class 'HondaEngine' through which we'll use the class object in the 'Honda' class above:

```
class HondaEngine

{

  public void start()

  {

    System.out.println("Engine has been started.");

  }

  public void stop()

  {

    System.out.println("Engine has been stopped.");

  }

}
```

Step#4

Now we have to build a class 'CompositionDemo' whereby we make a Honda class object and initialize it as follows:

```
class CompositionDemo
{
    public static void main(String[] args)
    {
        Honda h = new Honda();
        h.setColor("Black");
        h.setwheels(2);
        h.bikeFeatures();
        h.setStart();
    }
}
```

The output is as follows:

Bike color= Black   wheels= 2

Engine has been started

So what is the importance of composition?

You can be able to control other objects' visibility to client classes in composition and only reuse what you need.

Composition lets you create back-end class when it is required.

How Does Composition And Inheritance Compare?

My assumption is that you know how inheritance as well as composition compare, and want to know which one is the best to choose.

It is easier to change the back-end class' (or composition's) interface than a superclass (or inheritance). As illustrated in the previous example, changing the interface of a back-end class makes a change necessary to the front-end class interface provided that front-end interface stays the same. Conversely, changing the interface of a superclass can't just ripple down the hierarchy of inheritance to subclasses, but could as well ripple out to code, which only uses the interface of the subclass.

You'll also find it simpler to change the interface of the front-end composition/class compared to an inheritance or subclass. The same way superclasses are fragile, they can also be rigid. You cannot just change the interface of subclass without ensuring the new interface of the subclass is compatible with its super type. For instance, you cannot add a method that has the same signature to a subclass and yet it (the method) has a different return type as a method that is inherited from a superclass. On the other hand, composition lets you change the front-end-class' interface without affecting the back-end classes.

Composition lets you slow down the making of back-end objects unless and until they are required, and also altering the back-end objects throughout the front-end object's lifetime dynamically. Inheritance allows you to get the superclass' image in the object image of your subclass once the subclass is built, and it stays part of the subclass object throughout the subclass' lifetime.

You'd find it simpler to add a new subclass or inheritance that you'd find it to add new front-end classes or composition simply because inheritance has polymorphism. If you've got some code that depends on the interface of a superclass, the code can operate with a new subclass without changing. When it comes to composition, that is not true unless you are using composition with interfaces. When used together, composition and interfaces make very good design tools.

The explicit delegation or method-invocation forwarding composition approach will have a good performance cost often compared to the single invocation (in inheritance) of a superclass method implementation that has been inherited. Often here means that the performance entirely depends on many factors one of which includes how the Java virtual machine optimizes the program in the process of executing it.

With both inheritance and composition, altering the implementation of any class (and not the interface) is simple. The implementation change's ripple effect stay within the same class.

Selecting Between Inheritance And Composition

How do the comparisons between inheritance and composition assist in your design? The following are a few guidelines reflecting how I typically choose between inheritance and composition.

Ensure the inheritance models the relationship 'is-a'

The main guiding philosophy is that you should only use inheritance when a subclass *is a* super class. For instance, an orange likely *is-a* fruit, thus, I would most likely go with inheritance.

A good question you need to ask yourself when you think you have 'is-a' relationship is definitely whether the 'is-a' relationship is constant throughout the application's lifetime and, perhaps when lucky, the code's lifecycle. For instance, you could think that 'employee' is a 'person' when essentially, the term 'employee' denotes a role a 'person' plays only during a given period of time. What if the person is fired? What if he is a 'supervisor' as well as an 'employee'? When dealing with impermanent is-a relationships like these, you should consider that they have to be modelled with composition.

Do not just use inheritance to get code reuse

If you want to reuse code and that's all, and also there is no 'is-a' that you can see, you can use composition.

Do not use inheritance if all you want is to get at polymorphism

When polymorphism is all you want, and there isn't any natural 'is-a' relationship, you just use composition with interfaces.

Now, let's see how we can implement all we've learned in a simple project of building a   game in the next chapter:

Build A Simple Game With Java

The following guide will show you how you can make your own game in a simple step-by-step manner.

Before you begin, you need to install a program known as <u>Java</u> <u>processing</u> that is useful in building applications like the one we are going to build today. Just to explain a bit what it is, processing is open source and creates animations, interactive programs, drawings using basic syntax. It also includes the basic IDE that works as the interface for your programming. With Processing, you are able to create an extra abstraction to sort of mask particular Java's programmatic elements that an average beginner would deem difficult.

NOTE: abstraction lets you perform stuff with more ease especially when you don't have much background knowledge on the subject. If you were to build or process images in plain Java, you'd have a really painful headache.

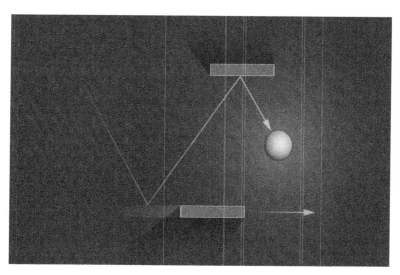

The game we are about to build in this section is some kind of combination of Pong, Flappy bird and brick breaker. I picked

this game particularly because it entails simple concepts and works to bring sense to others, which have been giving beginners a problem with regards to game development. You need to note that it is very difficult, first of all, to make complex games like platform games that have multiple levels, entities, players and so on. As we continue, you will see the way the code gets complicated really fast but the good thing is that it is generally well organized and simple. Just follow the piece slowly, making reference to areas in the book for concepts that need clarity, grab the entire code and play with it on your own as you begin pondering about your game soonest possible, and begin to implement it. Let's begin with the basics.

How To Build Flappy Pong
Initialize the different screens

We'll begin by initializing the project. First of all, we'll write the setup and draw blocks as anybody would normally do- so nothing new or fancy here! After that, we'll handle the various screens- these include the game screen, initial screen, game over screen and so forth. The question may arise though: how do you ensure the right page is shown at the right time?

It is quite simple to accomplish this task. We'll have a global variable storing the information of the screen that is active at the current time. We'll then draw contents of the right screen- this however depends on the variable. In the draw block, we'll include an 'if statement' which basically checks the variable and then presents the screen contents accordingly. Each time you want to change the screen, we'll change the variable to the screen you'll have to change the variable to the identifier you want displayed. That said, let's have an overview of how your skeleton code is:

```
/********* VARIABLES *********/

// We control which screen is active by settings / updating
// gameScreen variable. We display the correct screen according
// to the value of this variable.
//
// 0: Initial Screen
// 1: Game Screen
// 2: Game-over Screen

int gameScreen = 0;

/********* SETUP BLOCK *********/

void setup() {
  size(500, 500);
}


/********* DRAW BLOCK *********/

void draw() {
  // Display the contents of the current screen
  if (gameScreen == 0) {
    initScreen();
  } else if (gameScreen == 1) {
    gameScreen();
  } else if (gameScreen == 2) {
    gameOverScreen();
  }
}


/********* SCREEN CONTENTS *********/

void initScreen() {
```

Indeed, that may appear scary in the beginning but all I've done is create the basic structure and separate the different sections with comment blocks. As you can see, for every screen to display, we define a distinct method. In your draw block, you simply check the value of your variable 'gameScreen' before calling the corresponding method. When it comes to the part 'void mousepressed() {...}', you are basically listening to mouse clicks and in case the active screen is 0- the initial screen- you call the method 'startGame ()' which then begins the game as you would expect. This method's initial line changes the variable 'gameScreen' to 1—the game screen. When you understand this, the next thing you have to do is implement your initial screen. You will be editing the method 'initScreen ()' to do that. It goes like this:

```
void initScreen() {

  background(0);

  textAlign(CENTER);

  text("Click to start", height/2, width/2);

}
```

The initial screen now has a black background and a simple text reading 'click to start' that is right in the middle and aligned to the center. Nonetheless, when you click, nothing happens. You have not yet specified any yet for your game screen, the 'gameScreen ()' method does not have anything in it- which means that you are not covering the earlier contents drawn from the previous screen – which is the text- by having the first line of draw being 'background ()'. This is exactly why the text is still there, even though the line 'text ()' is no longer being called. For the same reason, the background is still black. We'll go ahead and start implementing the game screen.

```
void gameScreen() {

  background(255);

}
```

Once you complete this change, you'll notice the background turning white and the text disappearing.

Create the ball and implement gravity

We'll now begin operating on the game screen. We'll start by creating our ball. Right now, you have to define variables for its color, coordinates and size since you might want to change these values sometime later. For example, if you want to increase the ball's size as the player scores more so that the game is more difficult, you'll need to alter its size, so it has to be a variable. You'll define the ball's speed as well, once you implement gravity. Begin by adding the code below:

```
...
int ballX, ballY;
int ballSize = 20;
int ballColor = color(0);

...
void setup() {

  ...
  ballX=width/4;
  ballY=height/5;
}

...
void gameScreen() {

  ...
  drawBall();
}

...
void drawBall() {
  fill(ballColor);
  ellipse(ballX, ballY, ballSize, ballSize);
}
```

We have the coordinates defined as global variables, built a method that draw the ball, caked from the method 'gameScreen' but we had them defined in 'setup()'. The main reason for doing that is so that the ball starts from the left by one fourth and from the top by one fifth. I cannot give a particular reason as to why I want that but generally, that is a great point for the ball to start. Therefore, we needed to have the 'height' and 'width' dynamically on the sketch. 'setup ()' defined the size of the sketch, right after the first line. The 'height' and 'width' aren't set before the running of 'setup ()'

and that is why you could not do this if you defined the variables on top.

Gravity

On to the easy part: let's use a few tricks to implement the gravity- the following comprises the implementation first.

```
...
float gravity = 1;
float ballSpeedVert = 0;
...
void gameScreen() {
  ...
  applyGravity();
  keepInScreen();
}
...
void applyGravity() {
  ballSpeedVert += gravity;
  ballY += ballSpeedVert;
}
void makeBounceBottom(float surface) {
  ballY = surface-(ballSize/2);
  ballSpeedVert*=-1;
}
void makeBounceTop(float surface) {
  ballY = surface+(ballSize/2);
  ballSpeedVert*=-1;
}
// keep ball in the screen
void keepInScreen() {
  // ball hits floor
  if (ballY+(ballSize/2) > height) {
    makeBounceBottom(height);
  }
  // ball hits ceiling
  if (ballY-(ballSize/2) < 0) {
    makeBounceTop(0);
  }
}
```

<u>Click here</u> to see the expected result.

I'm sure you might be wondering whether your understanding of physics is being threatened. I know in real life, that's not how gravity works. Consider this to be simply an animation process. "Gravity", the variable, is only a numeric value- just a 'float' which makes it possible to use decimal values and not only integers- which, on every loop, we add to 'ballSpeedVert'. Actually, ballSpeedVert refers to the ball's vertical speed, which goes to the ball's Y coordinate (bally) on all the loops. You watch the ball's coordinates to ensure it remains in the screen and that if you don't (as you may know already), the ball will only fall to infinity. For now though, the ball is moving in a vertical direction only. This means that we watch the boundaries of the floor and ceiling in the screen. With method 'keepInScreen ()', we check whether 'bally' or + the radius is less than 'height' and in the same way, 'bally' or − the radius is higher than 0. In case the conditions don't meet, you get the ball to bounce (right from the bottom or top) using the methods: 'makeBounceTop ()' and 'makeBounceBottom ()'. We can have the ball move to the very location where it had to bounce and then get the product of vertical speed or 'ballSpeedVert' and -1 (note that the sign changes when you multiply with -1). when the speed value gets a − sign, it means that when you add the Y coordinate, the speed will then become bally−ballSpeedVert that's obtained from bally+(-ballSpeedVert). In this case, the ball changes its direction with that same speed immediately. Now, as you include 'gravity' to 'ballSpeedVert' and it has a negative value, it will begin getting close to 0, and eventually becoming 0 and then beginning to increase once more. This will make the ball to rise, then rise slower, stop and then begin falling.

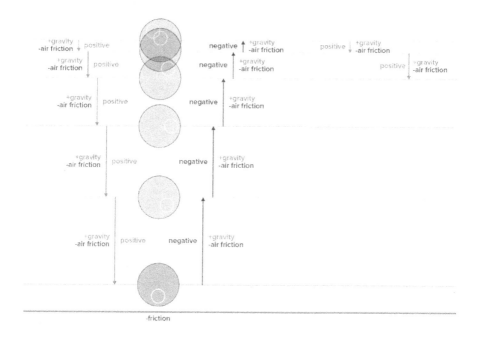

If you are keen enough, you'd notice that our animation process has a problem- the ball does not stop bouncing. If we used a real-world scenario to look at it, we'd say that the ball would face friction and air resistance each time it came into contact with a surface. That is exactly the behavior we want the animation process to have. Implementing that is pretty easy. Just add the code below:

```
...
float airfriction = 0.0001;
float friction = 0.1;
...
void applyGravity() {

  ...
  ballSpeedVert -= (ballSpeedVert * airfriction);
}
void makeBounceBottom(int surface) {

  ...
  ballSpeedVert -= (ballSpeedVert * friction);
}
void makeBounceTop(int surface) {

  ...
  ballSpeedVert -= (ballSpeedVert * friction);
}
```

The animation process will produce something like this.

'Friction', as the name suggests, refers to the surface friction; 'airfriction' on the other hand refers to friction of air. Obviously therefore, 'friction' needs to apply each time the ball comes in contact with any surface. Therefore, that is exactly what we did. The method 'applygravity ()' runs on every loop, you thus take away 0.0001 percent of its present value from ballSpeedVert on all loops. The methods 'makeBounceTop ()' and makeBounceBottom () run when the ball comes in contact with any surface. Therefore, we did the same thing in those method, only that we used 'friction' this time.

Now create the racket

You'll now require a racket which the ball will bounce on. You should also be able to control the racket. We'll make it controllable with a mouse. The code for that is as follows:

```
...
color racketColor = color(0);
float racketWidth = 100;
float racketHeight = 10;
...
void gameScreen() {
  ...
  drawRacket();
  ...
}
...
void drawRacket(){
  fill(racketColor);
  rectMode(CENTER);
  rect(mouseX, mouseY, racketWidth, racketHeight);
}
```

We defined the racket's width, height and color as a global variable. You might want to see them change during the game. We implemented the 'drawRacket ()' method, which does exactly what its name suggests. You have to set 'rectMode' to center so that the racket gets aligned to your cursor's center. Having created the racket, the next thing is making the ball bounce on it.

```
...
int racketBounceRate = 20;

...
void gameScreen() {

  ...
  watchRacketBounce();

  ...
}
...
void watchRacketBounce() {
  float overhead = mouseY - pmouseY;
  if ((ballX+(ballSize/2) > mouseX-(racketWidth/2)) && (ballX-(ballSize/2) <
  mouseX+(racketWidth/2))) {
    if (dist(ballX, ballY, ballX, mouseY)<=(ballSize/2)+abs(overhead)) {
      makeBounceBottom(mouseY);
      // racket moving up
      if (overhead<0) {
        ballY+=overhead;
        ballSpeedVert+=overhead;
      }
    }
  }
}
```

Click here for the result:

So, 'watchRacketBounce ()' ensures the racket and the ball collide. You need to check whether the ball and racket lined up horizontally and vertically. The initial if statement checks to see whether the X coordinate on the ball's right side is more than that on its left and vice versa. In case it is, the second statement will check whether the distance between the ball and the racket is equal or smaller than the ball's radius. If this conditions therefore meet, the method 'makeBounceBottom ()' is called and the ball bounces on the racket.

The variables 'pmouseY' and 'pmouseX' store the mouse coordinates at the previous frame. Since the mouse is able to move really fast, it is possible you might not detect the distance between the racket and the ball right between the frames in case the mouse is moving quickly enough towards the ball. Therefore, we take the difference of the coordinates of the mouse between the frames and consider that while detecting the distance. The quicker the mouse moves, the more distance is tolerable.

You also have to use 'overhead' for some other reason. We detect the path the mouse is moving my looking at the 'overhead' sign. If it's negative, it means the mouse was underneath in the last frame, which means the racket is going upwards. You want to increase the ball speed and a bit further than the regular bounce in order to stimulate the impact of hitting the ball using the racket. In case 'overhead' is below 0, you've got to add it to bally and also ballSpeedVert to have the ball move faster, higher. Thus, the faster the ball is hit by the racket the faster and higher it moves.

Moving horizontally and controlling the ball

We'll add horizontal movement to the ball here and then make it possible to control it horizontally using the racket.

```java
...
// we will start with 0, but for we give 10 just for testing
float ballSpeedHorizon = 10;
...
void gameScreen() {
  ...
  applyHorizontalSpeed();
  ...
}
...
void applyHorizontalSpeed(){
  ballX += ballSpeedHorizon;
  ballSpeedHorizon -= (ballSpeedHorizon * airfriction);
}
void makeBounceLeft(float surface){
  ballX = surface+(ballSize/2);
  ballSpeedHorizon*=-1;
  ballSpeedHorizon -= (ballSpeedHorizon * friction);
}
void makeBounceRight(float surface){
  ballX = surface-(ballSize/2);
  ballSpeedHorizon*=-1;
  ballSpeedHorizon -= (ballSpeedHorizon * friction);
}
...
void keepInScreen() {
  ...
  if (ballX-(ballSize/2) < 0){
    makeBounceLeft(0);
  }
  if (ballX+(ballSize/2) > width){
    makeBounceRight(width);
  }
```

Check the result <u>here</u>.

The idea is the same as that in the vertical movement. We created 'ballSpeedHorizon', a horizontal speed variable. We then created ballSpeedHorizon, a horizontal speed variable and also made a method that applies the horizontal speed to the ballx while removing air friction. Also, we added another two if statements to the method 'keepInScreen ()' that is meant to watch the ball for hitting the right and left screen edges. Lastly, we made sure the bounces from left to right are handled with methods 'makeBounceRight ()' and 'makeBounceLeft ()'.

Having added horizontal space to the game, the next thing is controlling the ball using the racket. The ball needs to move right based on the point on the racket that it hits. The racket edges should give it more horizontal speed:

```
void watchRacketBounce() {

    ...

    if ((ballX+(ballSize/2) > mouseX-(racketWidth/2)) && (ballX-(ballSize/2) <
mouseX+(racketWidth/2))) {
        if (dist(ballX, ballY, ballX, mouseY)<=(ballSize/2)+abs(overhead)) {

            ...

            ballSpeedHorizon = (ballX - mouseX)/5;

            ...

        }
    }
}
```

Here's <u>the result</u>.

What you did is determine the distance of the point the ball hits from the racket's middle using 'ballX-mouseX'. We then make it the horizontal speed. The difference isn't that much- I figured one tenth of the value is ideally natural.

Create the walls

We'll now add walls that move towards the left.

```
...
int wallSpeed = 5;
int wallInterval = 1000;
float lastAddTime = 0;
int minGapHeight = 200;
int maxGapHeight = 300;
int wallWidth = 80;
color wallColors = color(0);
// This arraylist stores data of the gaps between the walls. Actuals walls are draw
accordingly.
// [gapWallX, gapWallY, gapWallWidth, gapWallHeight]
ArrayList<int[]> walls = new ArrayList<int[]>();

...
void gameScreen() {
  ...
  wallAdder();
  wallHandler();
}

...
void wallAdder() {
  if (millis()-lastAddTime > wallInterval) {
    int randHeight = round(random(minGapHeight, maxGapHeight));
    int randY = round(random(0, height-randHeight));
    // {gapWallX, gapWallY, gapWallWidth, gapWallHeight}
    int[] randWall = {width, randY, wallWidth, randHeight};
    walls.add(randWall);
    lastAddTime = millis();
  }
}
```

```
void wallHandler() {
  for (int i = 0; i < walls.size(); i++) {
    wallRemover(i);
    wallMover(i);
    wallDrawer(i);
  }
}
void wallDrawer(int index) {
  int[] wall = walls.get(index);
  // get gap wall settings
  int gapWallX = wall[0];
  int gapWallY = wall[1];
  int gapWallWidth = wall[2];
  int gapWallHeight = wall[3];
  // draw actual walls
  rectMode(CORNER);
  fill(wallColors);
  rect(gapWallX, 0, gapWallWidth, gapWallY);
  rect(gapWallX, gapWallY+gapWallHeight, gapWallWidth, height-
(gapWallY+gapWallHeight));
}
void wallMover(int index) {
  int[] wall = walls.get(index);
  wall[0] -= wallSpeed;
}
void wallRemover(int index) {
  int[] wall = walls.get(index);
  if (wall[0]+wall[2] <= 0) {
    walls.remove(index);
  }
}
```

This is the result.

The first thing you need to note is the 'ArrayList', which is simply an implementation of the list and behaves like an Array. It however is resizable and contains great methods such as list.remove (index), list.add (index) and list.get (index). We store the wall data as arrays of integers inside the arraylist. The data we store in the arrays is meant for the gap in between 2 walls. Our arrays have these values:

[gap wall X, gap wall Y, gap wall width, gap wall height]

The actual walls are drawn according to the values of the gap wall. You need to note that these can be handled cleaner and better with classes. This is however how we'll handle it: we've got two base methods for management of the walls: wallHandler and wallHandler (). The latter adds to the arraylist new walls per wallInterval millisecond. We've got a global variable 'lastAddTime' that stores the last wall you added. In case the present millisecond millis () deducting the last millisecond added −lastAddTime- is bigger than the interval value −wallInterval- this essentially means that you have to add a new wall. Random gap variables then get generated according to the global variables defined at the top. A mew wall is then added into the arraylist and 'lastAddTime' set to the current millis (). The wallHandler () loops through the current walls that's in the arraylist and calls wallRemover (i), wallDrawer (i) and wallMover (i) for each item by the index value of the arraylist.

The wallDrawer draws the walls according to the gap wall data. The wallDrawer will usually grab the wall data array from arraylist before it can call the method 'rect ()' for drawing the walls to where they need to be. The wallMover takes the element right from the arraylist and alters its X location according to the 'wallSpeed' global variable. The wallRemover gets the walls off the arraylist, which are out of the screen. When a wall is thus removed from arraylist, this eliminates it from being drawn in all the following loops.

We now have to detect any collisions between the walls and the balls:

```
void wallHandler() {
  for (int i = 0; i < walls.size(); i++) {

    ...

    watchWallCollision(i);
  }
}

...

void watchWallCollision(int index) {
  int[] wall = walls.get(index);
  // get gap wall settings
  int gapWallX = wall[0];
  int gapWallY = wall[1];
  int gapWallWidth = wall[2];
  int gapWallHeight = wall[3];
  int wallTopX = gapWallX;
  int wallTopY = 0;
  int wallTopWidth = gapWallWidth;
  int wallTopHeight = gapWallY;
  int wallBottomX = gapWallX;
  int wallBottomY = gapWallY+gapWallHeight;
  int wallBottomWidth = gapWallWidth;
  int wallBottomHeight = height-(gapWallY+gapWallHeight);

  if (
    (ballX+(ballSize/2)>wallTopX) &&
    (ballX-(ballSize/2)<wallTopX+wallTopWidth) &&
    (ballY+(ballSize/2)>wallTopY) &&
    (ballY-(ballSize/2)<wallTopY+wallTopHeight)
    ) {
    // collides with upper wall
  }

  if (
    (ballX+(ballSize/2)>wallBottomX) &&
```

The method 'hWallCollision ()' is called for every wall on all the loops. You get the coordinates of the gap wall and calculate the actual walls' coordinates (from top to bottom) and then check whether the ball's coordinates are colliding with the walls.

Health and score

I don't know about you but I think we should have a health bar on top. When the ball touches the walls, it should lose health. This logic however doesn't make sense to have the ball bouncing back from the walls. When the health is 0, the game should end.

```java
int maxHealth = 100;
float health = 100;
float healthDecrease = 1;
int healthBarWidth = 60;
...
void gameScreen() {

  ...
  drawHealthBar();
  ...
}
...
void drawHealthBar() {
  // Make it borderless:
  noStroke();
  fill(236, 240, 241);
  rectMode(CORNER);
  rect(ballX-(healthBarWidth/2), ballY - 30, healthBarWidth, 5);
  if (health > 60) {
    fill(46, 204, 113);
  } else if (health > 30) {
    fill(230, 126, 34);
  } else {
    fill(231, 76, 60);
  }
  rectMode(CORNER);
  rect(ballX-(healthBarWidth/2), ballY - 30, healthBarWidth*(health/maxHealth), 5);
}
void decreaseHealth(){
  health -= healthDecrease;
  if (health <= 0){
    gameOver();
  }
}
```

The simple run is right <u>here</u>.

We made 'health', a global variable and then the method 'drawHealthBar ()' to draw two rectangles over the ball. The first one is the base health bar and the other one is the active one that displays the current health. The width of the second one is pretty dynamic and the formula healthBarWidth*(health/maxHealth) calculates it, the current health's ratio with respect to the health bar's width. The fill colors are now set based on the value of the health. Now for the scores:

```
...
void gameOverScreen() {
  background(0);
  textAlign(CENTER);
  fill(255);
  textSize(30);
  text("Game Over", height/2, width/2 - 20);
  textSize(15);
  text("Click to Restart", height/2, width/2 + 10);
}
...
void wallAdder() {
  if (millis()-lastAddTime > wallInterval) {
    ...
    // added another value at the end of the array
    int[] randWall = {width, randY, wallWidth, randHeight, 0};
    ...
  }
}
void watchWallCollision(int index) {
  ...
  int wallScored = wall[4];
  ...
```

```
if (ballX > gapWallX+(gapWallWidth/2) && wallScored==0) {
    wallScored=1;
    wall[4]=1;
    score();
  }
}
void score() {
  score++;
}
void printScore(){
  textAlign(CENTER);
  fill(0);
  textSize(30);
  text(score, height/2, 50);
}
```

We need to score whenever our ball passes through the wall.
We also need to create a maximum of 1 score per wall. This
means that in case the ball passes a wall and then goes back to
pass it again, there shouldn't be another added score. To do
that, we included another variable to the gap wall array inside
the arraylist. The new variable will store 0 in case the ball did
not pass that wall yet and a 1 in case it did. Then, we made a
modification to the method 'watchWallCollision ()'. We
included a condition which fires method 'score ()' and marks
the wall as having been passed in the instance the ball passes a
wall which it hadn't passed earlier.

The last thing we now have to do is have 'click to restart' implemented over the screen. We have to have all variables we used to their first value, and then restart the game:

```
...
public void mousePressed() {

  ...

  if (gameScreen==2){
    restart();
  }
}

...
void restart() {
  score = 0;
  health = maxHealth;
  ballX=width/4;
  ballY=height/5;
  lastAddTime = 0;
  walls.clear();
  gameScreen = 0;
}
```

We'll now add a few colors.

Success! We now have our very own flappy pong.

Conclusion

We have come to the end of the book. Thank you for reading and congratulations for reading until the end.

I truly hope you now have enough information about Java that you can use as a stepping stone for more learning.

If you found the book valuable, can you recommend it to others? One way to do that is to post a review on Amazon.

Click here to leave a review for this book on Amazon!

Thank you and good luck!

Printed in Great Britain
by Amazon

53991398R00102